S0-FAF-274

Canadian Gardening's
SMALL~SPACE GARDENS

By PENNY ARTHURS

with LIZ PRIMEAU *and* THE EDITORS *of* CANADIAN GARDENING MAGAZINE

&FENN

A FENN PUBLISHING COMPANY / MADISON PRESS BOOK

CANADIAN GARDENING'S
SMALL~SPACE GARDENS

ISBN 1-55168-290-7

A FENN PUBLISHING COMPANY / MADISON PRESS BOOK
First Published in 2005

All rights reserved
Copyright ©2005
Camar Publications Ltd. and
The Madison Press Limited

No part of this book may be reproduced or transmitted
in any form, or by any means, electronic or mechanical, including
photocopying, recording, or by any information storage and
retrieval system, without the written permission of the publisher.

The content, opinion and subject matter contained
herein is the written expression of the author and does not
reflect the opinion or ideology of the publisher,
or that of the publisher's representatives.

FENN PUBLISHING COMPANY LTD.
Bolton, Ontario, Canada

Distributed in Canada by

H. B. FENN AND COMPANY LTD.
Bolton, Ontario, Canada, L7E 1W2
www.hbfenn.com

Produced by

MADISON PRESS BOOKS
1000 Yonge Street, Suite 200
Toronto, Ontario, Canada
M4W 2K2

Printed in Singapore

Contents

Introduction

There's something about a small garden that makes me feel cozy and protected. I don't mean the tiny, fenced-in plots I've seen in the back of townhouses, graced only with grass or concrete pavers surrounded with a foot-wide border of petunias. I'm talking about spaces with a sense of purpose and design.

Before you can make a small garden that's both practical and inviting, you have to decide how you want to use it. Think of it as a room adjacent to your house. If what you really want is a low-maintenance place to drink coffee in the morning and host small dinner parties at night, you might consider paving over a really tiny space completely and investing in some stunning planters and a classic table and chairs in graceful wrought iron.

Or you could make your tiny property a complete garden in miniature — with a curved gravel path leading to a small bench beside a diminutive pond, and the rest of the space planted with perennials, herbs and some shrubs and evergreens for winter interest. A serious gardener/cook might turn a little backyard into a kitchen garden brimming with herbs and vegetables.

Whether you're grappling with a pocket-size city lot or a slightly larger suburban space, *Canadian Gardening's Small-Space Gardens* will help you through every stage of creating your own tiny perfect space — from planning your dream garden on paper to choosing the right plants, furniture, fencing and lights. Small spaces may be a challenge, but here's how you can make them one of life's little pleasures, too.

Liz Primeau, Editor
Canadian Gardening Magazine

CHAPTER ONE

THE ANATOMY *of a* SMALL GARDEN

*T*he quality
of a private haven is basic to the
idea of the small garden — a place to
experience peace and quiet, to breathe
air noticeably cleaned and cooled
by the trees and plants around us,
and, most important, to reconnect
with the natural order of
which we are a part.

SETTING *the* STAGE

S mall gardens are very *fin de siècle* — in this case, the twentieth — and chances are they will be a growing thing well into the new millennium. It's hard to imagine any feature of contemporary North American life that is more suited to our present needs and desires.

Home ownership, a degree of leisure time and disposable income have given ordinary people the luxury of creating a personal domain. And ordinary home owners do much the same as wealthy ones have always done — they change things to make them more comfortable, more fashionable and more expressive of themselves, their worldly success and their private dreams.

Recent home improvements have focused on generous kitchens for cooking, dining and living; on luxurious bathrooms for privacy or shared moments of indulgence — both early signs of that urge to stay home demographers call *cocooning*. The garden is the next logical thing, but it's not like the rest of the house. When it's done, it doesn't stay that way. In fact, it's not a thing at all; it's more like a new member of the family. It's demanding and rewarding and, in the end, it tugs you by the hand and heart and wins your passionate attention. What could be more perfect for all those baby boomers who are turning into empty-nesters?

Small spaces are right at the top of the gardening list because that's what most of us have — but also because they make sense. With most people working outside the home, with too much to do, too little time and no hope of hiring an army of paid garden hands, a modest acreage is both desirable and manageable. Nor is it just a second-best solution. Small can be a worthy challenge; small can be perfect.

It's also clear that compact living — and with it, gardening — encourages us to make better use of space; in so doing, we lessen the negative impact of our contemporary lifestyle on the world around us.

*A simple bench
set among voluptuous
roses and cool, green
foliage makes for perfect
peace in a tiny
Vancouver garden.*

In the end, though, the most telling reason for our preoccupation with gardens — particularly small gardens as places set apart — has less to do with social trends or demography and more to do with the inner self. Much as medieval walled gardens offered privacy and sanctuary from the ravaging hordes in harsh times long before our own, our personal plots promise refuge from the bustle and confusion of modern life. In urban jungle or suburban wilderness, these are sanctuaries for spiritual renewal, for connecting with ourselves, our friends and family. For marking significant life stages and for remembering 'that tree was planted the year that...' or 'those peonies came from my father's garden.' A quiet moment in the garden at the end of the day restores our sanity. As anyone who gardens will tell you, half an hour of hands in the soil is worth an hour on a psychiatrist's couch!

Getting *to* Know Your Space

The idealized notion of the small garden as a haven, a perfect vehicle for self-expression and the panacea for all modern ills may leave you a little overwhelmed as you look out at your own small slice of paradise. But with a nod to Lancelot Brown, mastermind of the grandest gardens of eighteenth-century England (and known as 'Capability Brown' for his insistence on the capabilities of any landscape), take comfort that no garden is beyond hope. All sites — however modest or ill-endowed — do have potential. The key to success lies in really understanding what you have and deciding what you want, in careful planning that accentuates the positive and does everything possible to banish the negative.

Before anything happens — before any plans are made — a garden must be given the critical eye. This is especially true of small spaces because they require you to do more with less. To take full advantage of everything the site has to offer, you have to understand the nature of the space and how it works. So, sit back and take a long, analytical look at what you have, starting with the physical realities — the anatomy — of the garden.

A scaled diagram or plan of your garden as it is now will help you visualize its size and shape, and understand just how much space you have to work with. It's also the best place to record your observations about the garden; by marking them right on the plan, you'll have them where they're most useful when you begin to plot your new scheme. If your lot slopes or changes level in some way, for example, you might think of creating a terrace with steps to a lower area; if you've noted a privacy problem, some sort of screening will probably be necessary. The more you notice and record on your diagram, the better you'll appreciate the problems and the potential of the site.

❧ Begin your voyage of discovery with the garden's boundaries and their relationship to the house. Note the size and location of all existing outdoor buildings and structures — from garage to gazebo. You may decide to work around these, or to move (or remove) them in your new scheme. Mark all the other built features you can't, or won't, change, such as a deck, steps or areas of paving. Pay attention to how the land rises or falls from the house, for any new design will have to acknowledge existing changes in level.

❧ Trees and large shrubs, both on the property and closely abutting it, are also an important part of the garden's structure. If you have mature trees, try to work with them; they are a gift from almost every point of view and, above a given size, are often protected by local by-laws. Shrubs can be transplanted, but it's often a perilous business. It may be better to plan around a glorious magnolia than to risk losing it. That said, the judicious removal of a tree or large shrub can sometimes open up brilliant new possibilities for a garden. Only by registering and reviewing each item will you equip yourself to make the right decisions.

❧ Small details are disproportionately significant because they can make impractical the changes you have in mind. Telephone wires, hydro and television cables have a habit of being in the wrong place, not to mention the underground services you inadvertently learn about by causing a minor explosion! Before you dig, check with your local utility companies; they will locate underground lines at no charge. Downpipes that empty water onto the surface, hose bibs, electrical outlets — all must be worked into your new scheme.

❧ Observe the conditions of the site, too. Drainage is crucial. There may be spots where water tends to collect and some re-grading will be necessary to create better run-off; other areas may be very dry, limiting what you can plant there. The nature and quality of the soil also dictate the gardening you can do, so check its pH factor and its friability. Is it nice and crumbly, with plenty of organic matter? Or heavy, sticky and in need of some sand, peat moss and humus? Note the passage of sun and shade through the garden at different times of day and through the year. In sunny patches, you might plant perennials, herbs or vegetables; dappled shade is ideal for sitting and dining; and much maligned deep shade can be transformed into a cool retreat or verdant woodland planting.

❧ Site conditions may also include things you can't see — chilling winds, frost pockets, traffic and noise pollution. Plan to minimize their effects and you can greatly enhance your enjoyment of the garden.

What about *the* garden itself?

As you work at discovering its many parts and understanding what is where, cast a more subjective eye over the character of your garden. Consider its less tangible qualities — its strengths and weaknesses, and how it relates to its setting.

❧ List the things you like about your garden — the mature brick wall of a neighbor's garage, some rockery stones or mossy paving, a fine shade tree or favorite clump of perennials. Re-use what you can to anchor your new scheme and to lend a sense of maturity until your new garden gets going.

❧ Look at views into the garden from the major windows of the house. Some may be good enough to emphasize as a focal point; others might be better camouflaged or screened out altogether. There may be good things outside the garden you can borrow visually and use to advantage — a long view, a lovely tree or an interesting architectural feature.

❧ Record the entrances and exits from the house to the garden and from the garden to what lies beyond. Note the most commonly used paths through the space — formal or otherwise — and the places you habitually sit. The way you have instinctively used the garden often suggests an appropriate layout, although sometimes fresh, critical thinking will suggest something better.

❧ Neighborhoods usually have a recognizable vernacular that might include the style and scale of its architecture and the building materials commonly used. Streets may be wide and gracious or narrow and eccentric; the whole area may be heavily treed with oaks or maples, or as open and flat as a prairie. It's not a matter of copying what everyone else has, but of discovering the local harmonies and working with them. A well-conceived garden enhances, and is enhanced by, its setting.

❧ It's important, too, to commune with the spirit of the place, that ethereal quality that expresses the quintessence of your garden — perhaps its wild and overgrown feel, its air of downtown sophistication, its privacy and enclosure or its wide-openness and fine vistas. Let the spirit move you, inspire you, train your eye and guide your hand.

A shady veranda connects house to garden in a small, carefully considered space where bold lines of paving and water set the tone.

Gardeners are enthusiasts, and enthusiasts often succumb to the urge to move full speed ahead, then learn on the job, reverse course, fix things up later, and wonder what went wrong the first time around. Resist. Delay. Look and look again. Only then will you truly see and understand things in all their charm and complexity — as a painting long perused, or a poem oft repeated. It is this understanding, more than anything else, that will inspire your vision, direct your planning and build your confidence.

MAKING *a* SCALED BASE PLAN *of* YOUR GARDEN

Use a scaled drawing to illustrate the exact proportions of your site and to help you add new things to your plan. Things that fit on a scaled plan will fit in real space, too.

❧ Scale down your garden to represent it on paper by using a smaller measurement to represent a larger one. For example, if 1/4 inch (6 mm) on paper = 1 foot (30 cm) on the ground, then steps 4 feet (120 cm) wide and with a run of 4 feet (120 cm) will be shown on the plan as a 1-inch by 1-inch (2.5 cm by 2.5 cm) square, and a shrub that grows to 6 feet (2 m) wide will appear on paper as a 1-1/2-inch (3.8 cm) circle.

❧ Look to official surveys and architectural plans for basic information, but be sure to check that they accurately reflect the realities of the site.

❧ Get someone to help you measure the site — this is a difficult job to do alone.

STEP-BY-STEP GUIDE

1 Use the house as your starting point or base line. Measure each face of the building. Accurately indicate doors, windows and other significant features — downpipes, air conditioning unit, etc. Scale this information onto graph paper. Be sure to leave enough space on the paper for the garden to be drawn in around it.

2 Measure out from the house to the property or fence line, first setting down the corners of the lot and their relationship to the house. In small, regular-shape gardens, start by establishing a point that is square to the house by running a taut line, flush with the side of the building, straight out until it meets the boundary. Measure the line and the distance from the line to the corner. Repeat the process all around the house, plot the information on your plan and connect the points.

3 Triangulation provides a more accurate way to record the location of things that are not directly in line with the house, as well as the relationship among the different elements of a garden. To precisely locate any feature — the corner of the lot, a tree or outbuilding — measure to it from two already established points such as corners of the house. On the plan, draw an arc with your compasses to the scaled equivalent of each measurement; the intersection of the two arcs represents the exact location.

4 Record all the garden's major features — trees, shrub masses, planting beds, structures — by eye and rough measurement. If your planning requires minute accuracy, use the triangulation technique to locate each feature.

5 To measure level changes, take a long, straight board of known length (say, 3 feet/1 m). Set it flat on the ground in the direction of the slope, with one end at the highest point. Using a spirit level to keep the board even, measure and record the distance from the far end of the board to the ground. This gives you the fall (say, 2 inches/5 cm) over the length of the board. Continue down the slope — each time extending the board from the last measuring point — and measure out and down, in a series of steps, until you reach the lowest point. Record each set of dimensions as you go. Tally all the measurements from board to ground to calculate the total fall across the given area. For example, the garden might slope 2 feet (60 cm) in all over 18 feet (6 m) from the house to the lot line.

6 To the basic plan, add all other site information. Indicate overhead and underground services, water and power sources, breather pipes, drainage problems and anything else that might limit your planning. Note the garden's good features and its shortcomings — pleasing views within the space and beyond it, areas of sun and shade, privacy/security problems and prevailing winds.

7 Use the base plan as the form around which you must order any changes you will make in the garden. Sketch new ideas on tracing paper used as an overlay to the base plan.

EQUIPMENT LIST

- Long tape for outdoor measurements
- Retractable steel tape for detailed measurements
- Clear scale ruler
- Set of compasses
- Circle template for adding plants to your plan
- Graph paper
- Large roll of lightweight tracing paper
- Plain lead and colored pencils

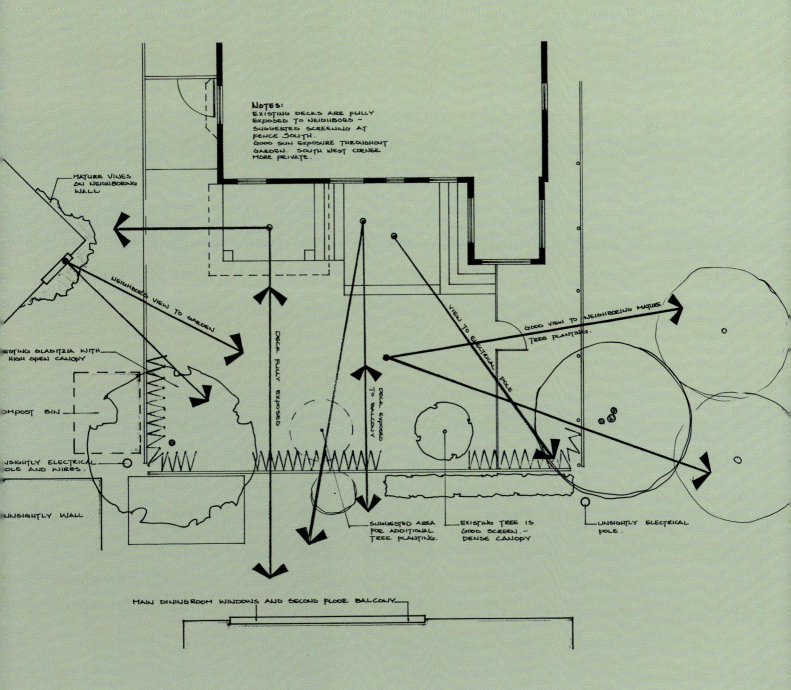

NOTES:
EXISTING DECKS ARE FULLY EXPOSED TO NEIGHBORS — SUGGESTED SCREENING AT FENCE SOUTH.
GOOD SUN EXPOSURE THROUGHOUT GARDEN. SOUTH WEST CORNER MORE PRIVATE.

MATURE VINES ON NEIGHBORING WALL

NEIGHBORS VIEW TO GARDEN

EXISTING GLEDITZIA WITH HIGH OPEN CANOPY

COMPOST BIN

UNSIGHTLY ELECTRICAL POLE AND WIRES.

UNSIGHTLY WALL

DECK FULLY EXPOSED

DECK EXPOSED TO BALCONY

VIEW TO ELECTRICAL POLE

GOOD VIEW TO NEIGHBORING MATURE TREE PLANTING.

SUGGESTED AREA FOR ADDITIONAL TREE PLANTING.

EXISTING TREE IS GOOD SCREEN — DENSE CANOPY

UNSIGHTLY ELECTRICAL POLE.

MAIN DININGROOM WINDOWS AND SECOND FLOOR BALCONY.

CHAPTER TWO

YOUR
own tiny
PERFECT
SPACE

*T*he notion of
tiny gardens as additional living space
serves well in the planning process.
Aim to accent the best features of your
garden and combine them with your
particular needs — as a single person,
a family, a budding gardener or
a gourmet cook. Then maximize
every square inch of space!

PERSONALIZING
a GARDEN PLAN

From Eden to Shangri-la, the idea of heaven as a wondrous garden is almost universal, but earthly garden delights are much more idiosyncratic and personal. Certainly, formal terraces and manicured lawns are adored and derided in equal measure, and one person's natural garden is another's weed patch.

Although your tiny corner of paradise must always take into account its setting and its resident spirit, it should also be especially *for* and *of* you. It should meet your needs in all the everyday, practical ways, and allow for the self-expression and flights of fancy that will make it uniquely yours. Successfully combining these qualities is at the heart of good design — particularly within the limited capabilities of a small space.

The practical things are easy, and a systematic and realistic look at the way you live will tell you almost everything you need to know. If you're a single working person, you might plan an evening garden for dining and entertaining. Low maintenance will be a priority if you spend a lot of time out of town. If you have young children, you'll need safe play space and storage for equipment and toys. If you love to cook, you'll want a garden filled with herbs and exotic salad greens. And if you have a home office, you might like to lug your laptop and cell phone into the garden on perfect summer days.

Self-scrutiny should not bring on an identity crisis — am I a working person or a vegetable gardener, or both? Still, thinking your way through how you'll want to use the garden does help the planning process. If you were renovating a kitchen, you wouldn't dream of having the appliances delivered before you'd decided where to put them. For some reason, this logic is often left behind when people move out into the garden.

Personal fancy is high on the list of what comes next. Inside the house, we're used to putting our individual stamp on things. We lavish great time and effort on color schemes, furnishings and artwork, all of which become distinctive expressions of self. Take the same intimate approach to your garden. Putting your special mark on a place is fundamental to a sense of sanctuary.

Because we have less experience in creating gardens, we're often tempted to adopt other people's visions — an image from a magazine or a recollection of a garden we've visited. Certainly, there's nothing wrong with borrowing inspiration here and there, but don't imitate too quickly or without being sure the idea will work for you. Just as you did when you were recording the anatomy and character of your garden space, look critically and seek to understand. Do crisp, formal lines show up in all the things you like — from gardens to interior decor to the clothes you wear? Or are you highly eclectic? Most people have a personal style, and that's what you should strive to express in your garden design.

Like many of the most important and distinctive parts of our character, taste and imagination are tightly bound up with memory. A prairie childhood will leave its imprint in a deep fondness for open spaces and sky. Stone, water and the scent of pine needles will resonate for those who spent childhood summers at the lake. When your garden is built around your own personal, internal landscape — the place that shaped you — it will truly be a place of your own.

In the meantime, remember that there are few shortcuts to inspiration. For most of us, it demands great effort — the tried-and-true design formula of looking, understanding and choosing carefully — but it also brings great reward. Collect thoughts, ideas and images that appeal to you; start a scrapbook and use it as a mirror to tell you what you like and feel comfortable with. And accept that in a small garden you can only do a few things effectively. Choose with care. Stay the course. This is the way to happy gardening!

Space, Scale *and* Illusion

The greatest design challenge of a small garden is to make a lot of what little you have. While there are no off-the-shelf solutions, there are tricks and techniques to help you grapple with the space to make it feel larger, more important and more interesting. These are particularly helpful as you begin to map out your new design.

❧ 'Keep it simple' is the cardinal rule of designing for small spaces. Take a strong idea and interpret it with finesse. Each part of the garden should count for something — the functional should look good, and what looks good should be functional.

❧ Make sure you explore and exploit the full extent of the lot. Often, the eye fails to grasp the potential of empty space, and you may find you have more room than you thought. Plan to occupy the whole area, taking paths and plantings right to the boundaries and into the corners. It obviously makes good sense to maximize usable space, but it will also make the garden seem larger. Use your base plan to assess these possibilities.

❧ Knowing the ideal size for new features you're planning helps to avoid wasting precious space or building things too small for comfortable use. Visit other gardens with a tape measure in hand and record the size and scale of things you see and like — how narrow a path, how broad a step, how wide an archway or gate, how large a deck or terrace for a table and six chairs. You'll soon get an idea of the right proportions for each element. By scaling them on your base plan, you can quickly see what's possible, and shift things around until you find a pleasing fit.

❧ The way you divide and connect the various parts of a garden can change the way it feels. Many small lots are long and narrow, or short and wide, but by using and manipulating strong lines in your design, you can change the way the shape is perceived. Horizontal lines across a bowling-alley lot — in the form of a path, structure, hedge or planting — push the side boundaries out and break the garden into a number of separate but connected spaces, each with its own pleasing geometry. Transversing the space this way also extends the physical journey through your garden, making it seem more spacious.

❧ Even in a tiny garden, it's possible to create separate rooms. Use a slender structure such as a lattice screen, a clipped hedge or a slight change in level to create finite spaces, each with a different mood and function. The variety of experience and the possibility of surprise make a garden more interesting and pleasant to use.

❧ Make a shallow garden seem longer by running strong lines out from the house to the boundary. The lengthened perspective is even

Paved surfaces and slender lattice screens define and separate spaces in a carefully articulated design where order and a sense of tranquility prevail.

more dramatic if a line narrows into the distance — a straight path with a slight taper, for example, or an allée of small trees planted closer together at the far end.

🍂 Lines that start strong and then disappear in a curve or behind a screen create an illusion of unending space, suggesting that the garden continues far beyond where the eye can follow. An ornament or open planting placed in the middle distance also suggests a greater expanse beyond.

🍂 Geometry is helpful in planning all sorts of gardens. It creates a framework for your design and suggests how best to arrange and connect its different parts. In the formal garden, whether traditional or modern, the lines remain strongly visible. Informal schemes are organized by the same rules, but the lines are softened and much less evident, particularly as the garden matures.

🍂 If you're lucky enough to have a slope on your property, make the best of it — changes in level make a garden much more interesting and foster the illusion of space. The slightest incline can be carved into a single step to emphasize the passage from one area to another. More substantial grade changes should be used to dramatic effect with generous steps, staged planting and open spaces at different levels. Don't waste a good grade change in a wishy-washy slope.

❧ Use bold, oversize elements and decorations to set up sizable expectations. Chunky fence posts, wide steps, large paving slabs, a single grand bench or one magnificent urn, magnificently planted, all suggest that this is a splendid place with plenty of room for large, striking things. Conversely, a multitude of tiny, fussy things in a small garden can underline its meagre scale.

❧ Clever use of color also misleads the eye. Bright, strong colors (reds and yellows) attract and distract — use them to draw attention away from a poor outlook and to keep the eye within the garden. Muted colors (greens and grey-blues) recede from view — use them to soften and push back the garden's boundaries and to suggest a misty and ever-receding hinterland.

❧ All good gardens, especially very tiny ones, should read as an extension of the house. Unless there is a good reason to do otherwise, the major axes of your plan should pick up the geometry of the house, not the lot lines, which are often irregular and would be better masked to disguise their limiting presence.

❧ To make indoor and outdoor spaces connect, use the same or complementary shapes, patterns and colors in both spaces. Flooring and paving designs might coordinate. Potted plants on both sides of a patio door help blur the point of transition from one realm to another.

❧ Put together a palette of the materials and colors you are planning to use to help you narrow your choices and keep things simple and coherent. This is common practice in interior design — it is equally relevant outdoors.

   Happily, garden-making does not stop at the drafting board. The lines you've drawn will become fences and paths; the geometry you've so carefully weighed will evolve into a terrace, lawn or water; scale and illusion will be transformed into the perfect tree or sculpture. It's important — and a relief! — to get out into the garden to check the rightness of what you're planning to do.

Interior and exterior spaces should flow together. Subtle shades of grey and bright florals are used in a treetop garden (right) to echo the color palette and style of an adjoining room. In a formal patio (inset), the garden is brought right to the house on vine-covered lattice panels in front of French doors.

CHAPTER THREE

PAVING, PATHS *and* STEPS

*P*athways,
steps and paving provide the
permanent form that makes
a garden pleasing to look
at and use all year round.
At their best, these hard surfaces
take on an almost sculptural
quality that sets the mood of
the whole garden.

THE IMPORTANCE *of* HARD SURFACES

Red brick paving defines the spaces in this informal, shady garden. Low brick and timber steps invite exploration of a further room set slightly above the main level. The lush planting includes a strategically placed Japanese maple specimen and smaller plants, such as the acid-green lady's-mantle in the foreground, to soften hard edges throughout the garden.

Even for blasé design professionals, there are magic moments in the making of a new garden. One of these happens the day the hard surfaces are defined. The bulldozer scoops out the shapes that soon will become paving, pathways and steps; the excavated cavities are filled with rough gravel and, presto, there lies the footprint of the whole garden. It may be weeks before the terraces, paths and steps are finished, but already the place is transformed — from nothing to clearly a garden in the making.

This moment of metamorphosis reveals just how important hard surfaces are. They create new and more intricate ways of occupying the garden. More than just places to sit or a way of getting from A to B, they are the bones of your design, the key elements that define and connect the spaces around which your garden will grow.

Plot the paved areas to carry through your design ideas and to mask the shortcomings of your lot. Use your scaled base plan, with all the site information marked on it, to help you work out the best spot for each feature you have in mind.

Your layout should be practical as well as visually pleasing. Paths must lead comfortably to and from places you need to go, and not meander aimlessly about. A terrace should be close to the house for convenient coming and going with trays of food and drink, and in an area of reasonable privacy. Thinking of the garden as additional living space helps you maximize its use and minimize its limitations.

As you rough in the different areas, balance open spaces of paving, lawn and water with things of greater mass such as a garden structure or major plantings. Aim to use the whole lot, to waste nothing and to create new divisions that make the journey through the garden interesting and surprising.

Material Choices

Well-detailed paths, paving and steps made of interesting materials are the hallmark of a classy garden. They are as important to a successful scheme as flooring and carpets are to interior spaces. Choose materials that reflect and enhance the mood and character of your setting — and keep things simple, for simplicity and harmony are key in small gardens.

It's important to find the right paving for the job at hand. A heavily traveled path, for example, needs a surface that's easy to walk on and durable enough to take abuse from the snow shovel. A dining terrace needs paving that's dense enough to support wayward chair legs. A woodland path, on the other hand, can be made of natural material such as wood chips, the better to encourage small plants to creep over its edges.

NATURAL STONE

Natural stone is the deluxe choice, although it's expensive and difficult to install. With its muted, natural tones and subtle texture, it's hard to imagine any setting in which it would be less than perfect. Flagstones are available in a wide range of types — sandstone, limestone, slate and granite — but it's usually best to stick with stone that is indigenous to your region, as imports often look out of place.

❧ Square-cut flagstone — the sort that comes with four straight edges — makes elegant, understated and functional paving. Laid with tight joints, it achieves an architectural, immaculate and almost weed-free surface that's ideal for a patio, dining terrace or heavily used pathways.

❧ Random-shape flagstone — the sort that's used for 'crazy paving' — is cheaper but trickier to lay because the idiosyncratic pieces have to be fitted together like a giant jigsaw puzzle. The finished product is softer and less formal, with spaces between the stones that invite invasion by mosses and other small plants. It's a good choice for less trafficked areas in tiny gardens where growing space is at a premium.

❧ Natural stone can be used in a multitude of different ways to achieve special effects. Straight-edged flags set in a definite pattern make a bold design statement. Large slabs and small fragments combine wonderfully in a textured patchwork quilt of paving. By varying the spaces between stones, surfaces can be made tight and functional where they are heavily used, while their edges blend softly into planting. Raised stones can be integrated into paths as natural steps, or into paving as built-in seating. In each case, the paving plan expresses the theme and character of the design.

BRICK

Brick is another pleasing paver. Warm, intimate and versatile, it's an excellent choice for tiny spaces because of its small unit size. It negotiates curves comfortably and makes light of difficult corners.

(Left) Square-cut natural flagstone makes an elegant yet functional floor in a sophisticated setting. (Right) In a more casual context, textured prefabricated concrete pavers combine with clay brick in a striking geometric pattern that is echoed in shadows cast by the pergola overhead.

🌿 Clay brick tends to be somewhat irregular in shape and have a rough surface which makes it feel very natural in a garden setting. Note, though, that only high-fired clay bricks are impervious enough to be suitable for paving. Interlocking bricks, made of concrete, are smoother and more regular, which makes them less organic but simpler to lay. Interlock is reasonably priced, comes in a wide range of colors and is highly durable.

🌿 The best thing about brick is the myriad charming effects it makes possible. Paths and paved areas can be finely articulated with different patterns, from herringbone to basket weave, and banding details that express the form and character of your design.

WOOD

Wood has some potential as a paving material, but is of limited durability. Sawn slices of a tree trunk, set in the ground as stepping stones, have an informal charm in a sylvan setting, but tend to be slippery when wet.

🌿 As an extension to a deck or for a walkway that crosses damp ground, a boardwalk path is a practical possibility. Somewhat elevated above soil level, boardwalks seem to float over the spaces they traverse — spaces that might be heavily planted or even part of a system of ponds.

🌿 Mixing board sizes and setting them in different directions — straight down, across, or diagonally to reflect the layout of the path — or wrapping the walk around a large stone or an existing tree trunk gives the customized look we seek in a small garden.

Square units of wooden decking are combined in a checkerboard floor that's ideal for a roof garden (right). For the rest of the deck, exposed aggregate pavers are set in the same square pattern.
In a much softer setting (inset), a gravel path winds invitingly between lavishly planted borders.

CONCRETE

Concrete is a very affordable option and by no means without potential for small gardens. Because you're working with comparatively small areas of paving, you can afford to finish it with considerable attention to detail.

🌿 Aggregates (gravel particles) added to the mix, and exposed by brushing while the surface is still damp, create great texture and tone. And as every kid knows, wet concrete cries out for all kinds of patterns and imprints — from signatures, hands and feet, to swirls, repeated geometrics and organic forms such as a leaf or shell.

🌿 Different-colored fragments of glass, pottery and rounded pebbles set in concrete make wonderful mosaics

that are great as an accent or detail, although perhaps a little rough underfoot for oft-used paving.

🌿 Expansion joints are a practical necessity to stop poured concrete from cracking, but you can turn them to advantage as a deliberate part of your design. Place them at regular intervals or in set patterns down a pathway or to delineate points at which a path changes direction or passes through a gate or under an arch. Bands of wood, brick or stone added to the expansion joints make an ornamental virtue out of necessity.

🌿 Homemade paving slabs provide another variation on the concrete theme. With an impressed pattern or mosaic inlay, they are truly an opportunity for self-expression.

GRAVEL AND OTHER MULCHES

Gravel and other surface mulches come at the end of the list because, of all paving options, they are the cheapest and easiest to install. They are, nonetheless, ideally suited to more casual settings — and certainly to most budgets.

❧ Gravel has great texture and crunch, but is not very durable. It must be set on a firm foundation of compacted crushed stone or screenings and be contained at all its edges with timber, on-end bricks or sections of flagstone set firmly in the ground. Gravel tends to get weedy, but a layer of filter cloth installed under the

foundation course will help control weeds coming from below. Airborne weeds are another matter, although they are less of a problem now that there are efficient and environmentally friendly herbicides, such as *Round-up*, to keep them down. To look really crisp, gravel needs frequent raking and occasional top-dressing.

❧ Organic mulches of shredded or chipped wood and bark replicate the forest floor and are perfect for woodland settings. They work well with all manner of low plants whose invasion in this context is welcome. They do decompose and need to be replenished often but their cost is comparatively modest, which makes them very useful as a temporary measure.

Steps are interesting to look at and to use, and their strong lines contrast well with the softness of growing things. These leisurely steps of timber and exposed aggregate make for pleasant passage in a lush garden in Vancouver. In the spirit of making more with less, the steps are also used to display an eclectic collection of planted pots and found objects.

FINISHING TOUCHES

A great way to achieve a custom look without breaking the bank is to add detail to comparatively economical paving with a small quantity of more expensive material. For some reason — and happily — one tends to notice the more luxurious parts and be less aware of the inexpensive ones.

❧ A finely detailed insert of brick or stone is the garden's equivalent of a richly textured rug. As the centerpiece of a small patio, a welcoming doormat at the entrance to the house or set inside an open garden structure, a small quantity of high-quality, interesting colored material enlivens expanses of otherwise lackluster paving.

❧ A 12-inch (30 cm) edging or banding of natural stone lifts commonplace interlock. Paving slabs set in a gravel path make it more decorative and more functional. Bargain-basement concrete pavers can be laid in a checkerboard design with good-looking clay bricks to define the squares. Japanese gardens feature exquisite blends of stone and pebble; the ancient Romans were masters of mosaic — the combinations are as wild and various as your imagination allows.

❧ Well-considered edges always pack a punch. Brick paths look much more substantial with a slightly raised soldier-course of the same brick set on end or dogtooth fashion. Open-work edgings of woven wire, cast iron or bent twig — inspired by the Victorian garden — are exquisite in the right setting. River stones, seashells, masonry fragments, even off-the-shelf concrete edging given a wash of color, will do the trick. These are small things, but they make a big difference in any garden.

Perfect Steps

Perfect paving deserves the perfect step, and steps can do wonderful things for a garden. They are interesting to look at and to use, and their strong lines contrast nicely with the softness of growing things.

❧ An almost imperceptible change of grade can be sculpted into a single step that will make the connection between two spaces much more dynamic — 5 or 6 inches (10 or 15 cm) is all you need.

❧ Make steps as wide and generous as your space allows and, if you have several steps together, be sure they are of uniform height. The proportions of a step are important, too — as the riser increases, the tread should diminish. Twice the height of the rise plus the depth of the tread should equal 26 inches (65 cms) is the magic formula. For comfortable and safe steps, make the risers no less than 4 inches (10 cm), no more than 8 inches (20 cm) and the treads no less than 9 inches (22.5 cm) deep.

❧ Wide, shallow steps are elegant and leisurely — they are ideal in situations where one is ambling from one space to another, taking time to look at plants and other minutiae as one goes. Narrow, taller steps, on the other hand, are more staccato and businesslike — they get you smartly from A to B without inviting pause. Steps should be as wide laterally as the path leading to them; where they give onto a soft surface, such as grass or organic mulch, a landing of harder paving material (probably the same as that of the steps) should be provided to prevent wear from the heavy footfall.

❧ Build steps to match or coordinate with the pavings you have chosen. Flagstone steps are elegant if the tread slightly overhangs the riser to form a shadow line. Brick risers combined with flagstone ease the transition from a brick house to the garden, while large stone slabs, flat boulders, 6-inch x 6-inch (15 cm x 15 cm) timbers and even heavy sawn logs are suitable in less formal settings.

❧ Remember that steps can make it difficult to move around the garden for people with limited mobility, or when you're using a wheelbarrow. If you think access is going to be a problem, consider incorporating a slender ramp into the fabric of your steps.

CHAPTER FOUR

FENCES, WALLS *and* HEDGES

*T*o keep the garden in and the rest of the world out, your small space will probably need an enclosure of some sort — a wall, a fence or a hedge. This structure is an essential part of the garden's architecture and it takes on special significance when space is limited.

THE BOUNDARIES *of a* SMALL GARDEN

All successful design combines form with function, and a well-planned enclosure should serve a purpose. It might conceal and shelter, frame a view or diffuse the line of vision, or perhaps be a combination of these. If seclusion is not an issue, you may not need a fence or hedge at all — minimal marking of the lot line with, for example, a chain strung between ornamental posts could be enough. You might decide you need some sort of screening inside the garden to divide spaces or to camouflage an eyesore.

Before you build, be sure you know what you need to achieve, and *caveat* gardener! — most cities regulate the maximum allowable height for boundary and screening structures. While good fences make good neighbors, excessively high ones don't.

The boundary fence in this Japanese-style garden combines form with function. Tall and opaque, it excludes the outside world — while its subtle, natural tones provide the perfect foil for both plants and the built parts of this tiny urban sanctuary.

But even a bit of wall adds substance and charm to a small garden. Brick or stone piers or short sections of wall, for example, add real panache and heft to iron or wood fencing that has a smaller price tag.

A low stone wall that separates spaces or retains different levels within the garden may be multifunctional *and* ornamental. While it brings form and character to your design, it can do lots of other things, too — serve as a table for your coffee tray or as casual seating, even provide a bonus planting opportunity for small, exquisite alpine plants that enjoy dry, stony conditions and can cascade down the face of the wall. Rustic fieldstone piles or ruined walls can be fun, too, and they definitely require less-than-perfect masonry skills. Covered with moss and ivy, they conjure up instant antiquity, a sense that someone was here long before you.

An old brick or stone garage — should you be fortunate enough to have one you don't need — can be transformed into wonderful walls. Leave two or three sides of the structure in place to form an outside room, or dismantle everything but one wall and re-use the extra brick elsewhere in the garden. Remember, though, that garage walls are not designed to stand up on their own — some sort of bracing will be necessary to make the remaining structure safe.

If you decide to take the plunge and build a new wall, give plenty of thought to the details. Choose building materials that are compatible with your house and consider how to use them most effectively. The stones or bricks can be set in a simple, regular design or in elaborate patterns with banding lines, recesses and fancy copings. Look for shapes and motifs that complement and reflect the architecture of your house. Remember, too, that a wall can take on any shape (straight, zigzag or curved, flat-topped, swooping or crenellated), which opens up great possibilities for your design.

Concrete or concrete block walls are not quite as expensive as stone or brick and can look great in the right setting. Their rather brutal nature can be softened with surface texture, patterned markings or insets of other

WALLS

Walls of stone or brick are the most luxurious of all garden structures. Solid and secure, they bestow an immediate sense of maturity and permanence, and their warm, natural tones and tactile quality are the perfect foil for plants. What's more, unlike most things, they only get better as they age. They're also very versatile, allowing for windows, peepholes, arches, doorways and all manner of ornamentation. Unfortunately, they're also expensive and not altogether the easiest project for the amateur builder.

Walls are the most permanent and versatile of garden structures. The stucco wall (left) incorporates an elaborate trimmed window that is both a pleasing ornament and a peephole to the landscape beyond. In another small garden (above), a low stone wall retains planting space and also functions as a multi-purpose bench, plant shelf and serving station.

complementary materials such as bands of granite or fragments of colored glass. Stucco adds a textured finish and comes in a wide range of colors you can use to achieve different effects — light, reflective shades to brighten a gloomy spot; soft, subtle hues to suggest the feel of natural stone; or a strong color such as terra cotta or blue that will establish the mood and color palette of the whole garden. Concrete walls are most effective as part of a bold design, in a garden with strong, simple plantings.

One word of caution. If you're building the walls yourself, make sure they're safe. Deep winter frosts will soon tip over any wall without proper foundations. All brick and concrete walls, high stone walls, or piers and columns need full foundations that go below the frost line — and that means digging deep. Low, dryset (unmortared) stone walls do not need full foundations, but should be built on a sturdy base of compacted gravel, with at least 12 inches (30 cm) of the wall set below ground level.

The finely detailed screen (left) combines basic lattice squares with a false-perspective design, mirror, a small sculpture and planting.

FENCES

From primitive palisades and split rails to New England pickets and French *treillage*, fences have long been a favorite way of keeping the world at bay. They may be more or less open, short or tall, plain and simple or highly sophisticated and ornamental — the choice is yours.

Today's fences reflect influences from great gardening cultures around the world, but none is more inspirational than Japan's, where the fence combines art, symbolism and tradition in forms of distilled perfection.

In Japan, each fence has a definite function. *Sode-gaki* or sleeve fences, so called for their resemblance to the sleeve of a kimono, are short, low structures that hang from a building to mask part of the garden from immediate view and to direct views from a given vantage point. In sophisticated locations, formal and finely

detailed structures are used; in rustic settings, natural styles prevail. Low, open fences beckon the visitor down the dewy path to the teahouse; but barriers are tall, solid and often roofed where intrusion is discouraged. Materials are carefully chosen and combined. In short, every detail is considered; there is a place for everything and everything is in its place. The lesson lies not in copying the style, but in observing what Japanese design seeks to accomplish and how thoughtfully it does it.

A fence that is simply *there* does little to enhance the garden it contains. Whatever sort of fence you build, add to its appeal with well-planned details and high-quality construction.

❧ At the least, you must make a conscious decision about the size of the boards you use, their alignment and spacing. Wide boards make a strong, simple and unobtrusive fence; smaller boards, used in a definite pattern, make a design statement — which may be desirable in a very small space with scant opportunity for decorative flights of fancy. Consider setting the boards in diagonal or vertical patterns, perhaps using a different configuration for alternate panels. Slightly different fence styles that are variations on a single theme nicely characterize and define separate rooms within a single garden.

❧ In small spaces, little things mean a lot. Straight, solid top and bottom rails, bracing pieces that are placed by design rather than chance, boards or lattice panels held neatly in place by nailing strips — all these details make for a quality look. Battens covering the spaces between vertical boards and decorative mouldings used in place of simple nailers add an extra touch of class.

❧ Lattice, a close descendant of elaborate French *treillage*, has recently made a big comeback. Available off the shelf in different shapes and densities, it is one of the better prefabricated materials around.

❧ Ornamental lattice panels mounted on a wall or solid fence become a textural surface relief with depth, plays of light and, of course, the potential to support foliage and flowers. As a device to give instant interest to a barren surface or to dress up your side of someone else's indifferent fence, surface-applied lattice is hard to beat.

❧ Fancy lattice screens are equally wonderful — both in themselves and for the way they filter light and cast ever-changing patterns of shadow. Open fences of this sort are less dominant than solid boards. They allow the passage of air and light and are ideal if you crave both a feeling of privacy and full value from the landscape that lies beyond.

❧ Richly detailed lattice is particularly striking, and customizing your own *treillage* affords the luxury of *à la carte* design. It requires little special equipment and is one of the easier do-it-yourself building projects for the gardener with a creative bent. For the fainter of heart, a mix of prefabricated lattice segments can produce a good, though less complex, substitute. Combine diagonal and square, or open and privacy-grade, pieces in a multi-panelled screen — perhaps using a dense, square pattern for the border and an open, diagonal one for the center. Inexpensive lattice, by the way, always looks better when it's painted to mask its imperfections.

BUILDING A FENCE

❧ Sturdy posts are basic to a fence that stands up. Whether they're made of pressure-treated timber or a durable untreated wood such as cedar, they should be set deep in the ground and preferably in concrete.

❧ To avoid bowing and buckling stringers (the supports that run top and bottom between the posts to carry the fence boards), use nothing smaller than 2-inch x 4-inch (5 cm x 10 cm) timbers and set your posts no more than 8 feet (2.6 m) apart. Fence panels over 4 feet (120 cm) high will need additional horizontal support in the form of a third stringer set in the center of the fence, to keep the boards flat and straight.

❧ Make your fence as sturdy as your pocketbook and the site allow. 6-inch x 6-inch (15 cm x 15 cm) posts are ideal, but smaller posts (4-inch x 4-inch/10 cm x 10 cm) may be boxed or built out on all four sides to make them look more substantial. And remember that fence posts offer plenty of opportunity for embellishment — from beveled corners and moulded caps to surface relief decoration and fanciful finials.

Before You Build

❧ Early in the planning process, note prevailing winds and sun patterns in the garden.

❧ Solid boundary structures may affect the ecosystem of your garden by casting excessive shade or limiting air movement. Where winds are strong and persistent, they may cause downward turbulence that increases wind speed and chill on the leeward side.

❧ In such situations, choose hedging, open fencing or pierced walls that filter rather than block the wind. Open structures are also more suitable for very tight spaces with poor air circulation.

❧ Fences that combine solid board with a topping of lattice provide privacy without a feeling of being excessively closed in. But how often this good fencing idea is marred by poor proportions! The key to a good-looking lattice/board combo is getting the two elements in a pleasing balance. One-third lattice to two-thirds solid board is about right. Instead of lattice, you might top your fence with horizontal or vertical pickets if they sit more comfortably with your design.

❧ Picket fences that began life as utilitarian rustic structures are most familiar to us in their more elaborate Georgian and Victorian forms. They are not effective privacy fences, but their scale and ornamental character make them good candidates for small gardens where seclusion is not important. They are open, friendly fences, perhaps best used in the front garden where they add great curb appeal, framing the house attractively and inviting the visitor to enter. They also combine well with climbing or rambling plants, such as roses, or with neatly clipped hedges. Note, though, that picket fences have a very distinctive style and should only be used where they're compatible with the house and the local architecture in general.

❧ And what about high-tech? Garden style through the ages has reflected the technology of its time. Cast-iron fences, for example, became popular when the Industrial Revolution made them widely available. In our own time, gardeners seem more inclined to borrow from the past than to design with the modern industrial materials of contemporary architecture. Although small-space gardeners may be limited by the size of their lot, they might extend the boundaries of imagination by using some of these materials. Wire mesh, industrial piping, heavy-duty cables and fasteners might make post-modern fencing that would be just right in certain urban settings.

TROMPE L'OEIL

There are design conceits — or deceits — that elevate ordinary garden walls and fences far above the mundane, and many of these are perfect devices for the small garden.

Some are accurately described as *trompe l'oeil* (trick the eye) because they fool us into believing something to be other than it is — a space larger, a property more extensive, a setting more secluded than it really is. False gates that lead nowhere, windows or *clairvoyée* that look upon a view that might be (but, alas, is not) one's own, opaque lattice screens with a disappearing perspective — all these work well in small gardens. And even after you have discovered their trick, they remain interesting, decorative and fun.

❧ These illusions can be achieved by using real structures — an interesting old door, an iron gate, an old window frame, an antique grate set in a wall or fence — or they can be totally *faux* images. Any of these features, even walls and fountains, can be painted onto fence panels. The most elaborate and fanciful interpretations of the form are murals or painted perspectives that allow unlimited opportunity for personal expression and may even fool the more credulous visitor. For the less intrepid artist-gardener, stamped or stenciled decorations are a good alternative. Ivy leaves, clusters of grapes or wisteria blossoms, Greek key and gingerbread designs are available at quality paint stores.

*A well-placed mirror trompe l'oeil (right) makes limited space seem limitless as it reflects and projects the garden setting of table, fence, statue and trees.
In another garden (inset), a painted faux-stone wall carries a lion's head mask and lavabo basin.*

Mirrors are another popular and elegant way to achieve illusions, but they must be handled with care. There's little point in placing a large mirror to reflect a perfect view of the compost heap. Before you take the plunge, carry a mirror out from the house to find a spot where it will indeed enhance and entrance. Use a heavy-duty, weatherproof mirror and frame it between two handsome columns, in a lovely arch or in an old finely detailed doorway, just as you would a picture — and keep the *Windex* close at hand. Nothing is more miserable than a spattered and streaky mirror that fools no one.

Some wall or fence ornaments are designed not to fool but merely to please. Niches and shelves bearing potted plants, pieces of sculpture or any other interesting collectibles enliven a garden, as do masks and friezes, lanterns and hanging pots brimming with flowers or foliage. In very tiny spaces, garden tools can be stowed in an interesting old cabinet mounted on the fence or hung from large wooden dowels or antique hooks in an original but utilitarian collage.

From the serious and expensive to the most simple, these are all imaginative ways of making your garden look great.

HEDGES

Hedges are a striking alternative to walls or fences in small gardens where vertical surfaces inevitably dominate. They define the form of a design and provide year-round interest. Other plants may be more eye-catching during the summer months but, in winter, hedges shine as principle players on the gardening stage.

Hedges are also functional, filtering wind, pollution and noise, but like all the growing things in your garden, they do need time — time to mature, and your time to keep them neatly clipped and under control.

Evergreen hedges are hard to beat. In small gardens, they will probably be close-clipped to limit their girth, but their height can be as great as your patience and your neighbors will allow.

White cedar (*Thuja*, Zone 3) and yew (*Taxus*, Zone 4) are both excellent choices. They look beautiful and tolerate heavy clipping. When you buy either for a hedge, make sure you purchase a variety that has the potential to achieve the shape and height you need.

Cedar is a lively green and needs sun. It takes on a rugged and informal look as it matures, making it ideal for less formal gardens with a country feel. Yew is a dark, matte green and grows in both sun and shade. It looks right anywhere and is extraordinarily tolerant of being sculpted into almost any shape. One of the garden's most architectural plants, yew can easily be trained and clipped into arches, windows or niches and all manner of whimsical shapes. If leaping deer are your fancy, yew's for you — although, at the limit of its range, you may need to give it protection from winter winds.

Some broadleaf evergreens also make fine hedges. Holly (*Ilex*, Zone 6) and Oregon grape (*Mahonia aquifolium*, Zone 4b) both make lovely, informal hedges; both are shade-tolerant and their glossy leaves bring a splash of light to the dullest corner. Euonymus — especially 'Sarcoxie' (*E. fortunei* 'Sarcoxie', Zone 5) — though usually thought of as a creeper and climber, is woody enough to make an excellent hedge. Start it off on a framework of timbers or strong wires and it will soon form a satisfying hummock that can be clipped as closely as your look requires.

Box (*Buxus*, Zone 5), a broadleaf evergreen with small, shiny leaves, is traditionally used for the low, closely clipped hedges that form the knots of a *parterre*, the neatly enclosed beds of formal European gardens.

Low box hedges have long been a feature of formal European gardens. In this crisply designed Canadian garden, box hedging defines carefully sculpted paving and neatly contains the clipped shrubs and colorful annuals.

This versatile plant performs just as well in small contemporary spaces as an edging device for a path or lawn (see photo, p. 45), or as a low, understated partition. In ideal settings, box grows much taller if left unclipped (some Italian gardens have box hedges over 15 feet/5 m high) or it can be shaped into interesting forms either as part of a hedge or as a single specimen. Box, like yew, may need winter protection at the limit of its range.

❧ Deciduous hedges
are a striking addition to a small garden. They may not be green in winter, but their seasonally changing character can be viewed as a plus.
❧ Beech (*Fagus sylvatica*, Zone 6) and privet (*Liustrum vulgare*, Zone 5b) both make attractive, tall hedges that clip easily into clean, crisp lines.

Dwarf lilac (Syringa meyeri 'Palibin') with allium.

❧ Peking cotoneaster (*C. acutifolia*, Zone 2) and the Manchu cherry (*Prunus tomentosa*, Zone 2) both make excellent clipped hedges for cold regions. Cotoneaster, with its small leaves and persistent fruit, maintains a narrow, upright habit, while the Manchu cherry displays tiny pink-white, fragrant flowers in spring and interesting shiny reddish-brown, exfoliating bark in winter.
❧ Soft, unclipped hedges are equally lovely, though they need more space to spill about. Almost any reasonably sized shrub is suitable as long as its growth habit allows it to blend with its neighbors. Be sure that it has a decent winter form and pleasing foliage, for flowers are usually fleeting. Bridal wreath (*Spiraea* X *vanhouttei*, Zone 4) is a

Privet has small, somewhat shiny leaves and a winter look that is interesting when covered with frost and snow. Beech is larger and needs more room, but it's still an excellent choice for the small garden, not least for its stellar year-round performance. In spring, the new green or copper leaves unfurl like the wings of a butterfly fresh from the cocoon; through the summer, they keep their color well and rustle pleasingly in the breeze; in fall and winter, they dry to a marvelous paperbag-brown, only to fall as new leaves emerge in spring.

good choice; it has a blue-green tumbling appearance in leaf, and dazzling white blossoms for a brief period in early summer.
❧ Dwarf lilac (*Syringa meyeri* 'Palibin', Zone 2b), with masses of highly perfumed mauve flowers, makes a very charming small hedge (just over 3 feet/1 m) that stays compact and neat through the growing season. The many varieties of potentilla, flowering throughout most of the summer in shades of yellow, orange, pink or white, also make attractive low informal hedges.

Roses are excellent candidates for informal hedging. The tough species roses, such as rugosa (*Rosa rugosa*, Zone 2) and hybrids like Jens Munk (*Rosa* 'Jens Munk', Zone 2), make fine hedge material because they are easy to care for and have a fuller, more leafy appearance than more cultivated roses.

In the toughest situations, peashrub (*Caragana arborescens*, Zone 2) is the answer. Brought to Canada by Prairie settlers to use as a windbreak, it makes a dense, rather wild, but not unappealing hedge with shiny green leaves and attractive, pea-like yellow flowers in June. Caragana, which grows to a height of 10 feet (3 m), can also be clipped into greater discipline and to limit its size. For a low hedge, choose the pygmy peashrub (*C. aurantiaca*, Zone 2).

A hedge of lush pink roses adds to the prettiness and the privacy of this tiny garden.

second, living layer atop a fence or wall where greater height is needed. Pleached hedges, by the way, are definitely for the dedicated gardener in search of a new challenge.

While it is appropriate to think of hedges as part of a garden's architecture, it's also important to remember they are part of its horticulture and must be nurtured. Set them in well-prepared trenches and feed and water them as any other shrub or small tree. Treat evergreen hedges to a hose-down once in a while, especially in early spring, to wash away winter's grime.

Make sure you know how and when to prune your hedge. Cut back informal hedges after planting to encourage new, low growth. As the plants get established, prune after the main flush (or flushes) of growth for non-flowering hedges, and after flowering for those that bloom. Clip formal hedges immediately after planting to promote thick growth and to establish a level crown. They should taper to the top to allow light to reach the sides, water to penetrate to the base and to stop them from getting top-heavy, especially when they're covered with snow. Use clippers only for architectural hedges; soft hedges must be pruned branch by branch, like a shrub.

Pleached Hedges start high and go higher! Although we usually think of a hedge as a dense, mounded planting that starts close to the ground and creates a barrier up to and just above eye level, a pleached hedge is made from the branches of single-stemmed trees — such as linden (*Tilia cordata*, Zone 3) or hornbeam (*Carpinus betulus* 'Fastigiata', Zone 5) — that are trained and interwoven to form a screen on stilts. This treatment offers space below and privacy above, which is ideal for some small gardens. It can also be adapted to form a

CHAPTER FIVE

GARDEN STRUCTURES *and* DECKS

*F*rom a simple
archway to an elaborate gazebo, garden structures
add form, detail and character to a small garden
and offer wonderful opportunities for creative vertical
planting. Above all, they contribute to the privacy
and seclusion that are so fundamental to the idea
of small, personal spaces.

STRUCTURES
in a SMALL GARDEN

*Garden structures
may be as simple as
an archway (left)
that frames a view of
something lovely
in your own garden
or beyond.*

The earliest garden structures were no more than simple agricultural forms built to support fruiting vines, but humankind soon learned to enjoy the shade and seclusion they provided. As architecture and landscape design developed beyond the merely functional, garden structures also became more elaborate and decorative, and were contrived purely for pleasure.

Structures in the garden can be as minimal as an arc of bent twigs over a bench, or as complex as a summerhouse replete with roof, windows and a door. They can be purely ornamental or as functional as an outdoor room for sitting, eating and entertaining. Whatever your fancy, don't just buy an idea off the shelf. Go for something that really fits the site, that works with your theme and carries through the objectives of your design.

ARCHWAYS, PERGOLAS *and* ARBORS

Archways, pergolas and arbors are open structures that span something — a path, a bench, a seating area. They combine architecture and planting (to a greater or lesser degree) in a form that reinforces the layout of the garden, and they bestow a sense of enclosure without excessive bulk.

❧ Starkly sculptural or luxuriantly planted, this sort of structure can frame a view within the garden or the vista that lies beyond; it can also provide privacy and create areas of light and shade that make the garden interesting and pleasant to use.

❧ However modest, arching forms afford the inexplicable pleasure of walking under something — a remnant of childhood? — and the excitement of emerging from a shady enclosure into bright, open sunlight.

SUMMERHOUSES *and* GAZEBOS

Summerhouses and gazebos are more substantial structures, usually with a roof and sometimes with solid walls. They are a destination in the garden, rather than part of the journey through it.

❧ A simple, vine-covered gazebo of rustic timbers or open lattice makes a delicious

retreat from the heat of day, while a summerhouse might be set up as an outpost of home. Outfitted with lights, power, even a phone jack, it can become a studio, a teenager's retreat or a home office just a little removed from the tyranny of domestic chores.

❧ Usable buildings of this sort also add an interesting dimension to one's experience of the garden. They are places to sit and to look at things from a different perspective. Rather than viewing the garden from the house, as we do most of the time, we can contemplate the house from the garden.

❧ Even in a tiny yard, a summerhouse is not out of place; it simply becomes the organizing feature of the whole scheme, an integral part of the garden and not something subtracted from it. Whatever open space remains serves as a transitional courtyard where the

The roofed pavilion (left and below) is both ornamental and functional. It stands as the focal point of this small city garden, provides shade and shelter for the hot tub and is a perfect spot from which to view things from a different perspective.

mood changes from the comparative formality of indoors to the more casual atmosphere of an outpost — and where, as the famed English gardener, Gertrude Jekyll (1842-1932), put it, "more gentle employments can be enjoyed in a garden atmosphere."

STORAGE SHEDS

Storage sheds are structures, too, and should be accorded the same care and attention as their more decorative cousins — especially in a small garden where function and ornament should never be far apart.

❧ One approach is to use the side of the shed that faces the garden as a backdrop for something else — perhaps a *trompe l'oeil* or a built-in seat framed in lush foliage. Interesting windows and window boxes are a pleasing addition.

❧ If your space is so tight that the entrance to the shed must remain fully visible, consider a wonderful old door (perhaps a split barn-type door) set under an arch of roses. Once a shed — now a veritable jewel-box!

The blank face of a storage shed is transformed into a striking backdrop for a paved seating area flanked by privacy screens of open lattice.

BEAMS *and* TIMBERS

Beams and timbers that span small spaces can barely be considered garden structures, but they do excellent duty providing shelter and privacy in a tight spot.

❧ Beams extending from the house to a boundary fence only a few feet away, and covered with luxuriant vines, transform an awkward eyesore into a pleasing tunnel of green that opens into the light of the garden.

❧ Beams that form an open pergola out from the back of a house, or a shallow eye-lid arbor over a very sunny window, provide shade and privacy, dress up a dull façade and bring the garden right up to the house.

TENTS *and* AWNINGS

Tents and awnings are not garden structures at all, but they can do a lot of the same jobs.

❧ A retractable canvas shade over a patio door, an open-sided tent, a large parasol or just an outdoor drape that can be drawn to close off part of the garden for private entertaining — all provide shade and shelter, exclude prying eyes and create atmosphere. They're especially handy if your garden is on property you rent or lease.

PLANTS

For the patient and diligent gardener, it's possible to create garden structures entirely of plants.

❧ Woody vines and some trees and shrubs can be trained and pruned around a minimal structure of wood or heavy wire that becomes less visible as the plants mature. Ancient wisteria walks, apple arches and laburnum tunnels are remarkable in bloom and equally intriguing in their form long after the leaves have fallen.

A structure is handily defined as "any assemblage of materials intended to sustain loads," and it goes without saying that it should do so without risk to life and limb,

or the possibility of leaning, sagging or buckling. Home gardeners should take seriously the engineering of any structure. Use materials that are strong enough for the job, with plenty of support for horizontal parts — if in doubt, add more. Set all posts firmly in the ground, as you would for a fence, and use fasteners that won't rust. Building right the first time guarantees you'll avoid the depressing experience of having to rip down wonderful, mature vines to do running repairs.

DECKS
for SMALL
SPACES

Decks belong to both the house and the garden. They are transitional structures that, at their best, provide a comfortable, convenient, low-maintenance space for outdoor living. Too often, though, they are thrown up as cheap and cheerful landscaping that presents as many problems as it solves. When decks are built high off the ground, they create serious privacy problems and isolate one of the garden's most intensely used areas from the pleasures of green and growing things.

If you settle on a deck as one feature of your plan, be wary of these pitfalls. Be sure you are making the best use of the limited room you have and consider not only the shape of the structure but also the negative space around it. It's better to take decking right up to the boundary than to leave an isolated ribbon of unusable ground.

The deck in a Japanese-style garden (above) performs as transitional space, a dining area and the perfect vantage point from which to enjoy the well-chosen palette of plants.

❧ You might lower the deck floor by setting it several steps down from the main storey of the house; this will put you closer to the garden and farther away from your neighbors. If you have enough room, think of gently terracing the deck into several connected tiers and building the garden up around it.

❧ In a very tiny space where the exit from the house is well above grade, decking over the entire garden might make sense. This allows maximum use of every inch and is a quick way of banishing old landscape features that

are difficult and expensive to remove. Existing trees with a well-defined trunk can be built into the deck — as long as you leave plenty of room for future growth and for moisture to reach the tree roots. If the deck is low enough, integral planters can be built from the ground up to allow larger plants to set root right in the earth, making them less vulnerable to the extremes of climate.

❧ Use your ingenuity to make the flat plane of the deck more interesting. Wide boards (perhaps 2 inches x 6 inches/5 cm x 15 cm)

are best for large decks; whereas very narrow slats (2 inches x 2 inches/5 cm x 5 cm) make a finely textured surface, suitable for smaller expanses and steps. Set the boards in a simple linear pattern to emphasize one dimension over another, in concentric squares or in repeating blocks like parquet.

Decking can play a part in organizing the flow of movement through a garden. Here, well-detailed steps from a slightly raised platform establish two distinct directions and routes through the garden to maximize the use of very limited space.

A fascia board around the exposed edges of the whole structure makes for a clean finish, and you can close off the underside with framed-up panels of lattice, horizontal or vertical laths or even chicken wire that will entice climbing plants to produce a quick cover.

❧ The empty space under decking makes great storage for things like the spare hose, plant pots and children's toys. Remember, though, that whatever you put there will be open to the elements and consigned to permanent burial if access to the space is difficult.

FINISHING TOUCHES

Safe railings are a must for high decks and, in most places, they are required by law — something you should check before you start to build — but railings can and should look good, too.

❧ Make the corner posts that support the railings big and strong to provide stability and visual weight, and choose a pattern that works with the style and period of your house. Build the top rail wide enough to carry a glass or support lingering elbows, expand it even more to contain a shallow planter box for a luxuriant show of annuals.

❧ Railings of wrought or cast iron are obviously wonderful in the right setting, but they require deep pockets. Cheaper thrills are available to anyone with a sense of whimsy and an eye for found art. Pieces of antique iron railing, old heating grates or turned wood pickets (preferably with peeling paint), even pieces of driftwood add pizzazz to otherwise ordinary railings.

❧ Barbecues — often large and less than lovely — should be planned into your scheme early in the process. Locate them safely, conveniently and where they have minimal visual impact. Storage for cooking utensils and other things can be incorporated into seating or under shallow planter boxes.

❧ Planters and seating that are a permanent part of the deck's structure should be consistent with the overall design you've chosen. Think of them as fixed furnishings and plan them with an eye for detail. Planters might be faced with smooth tongue-and-groove wood, framed panels of lattice or decorative mouldings.

❧ Once the construction is finished, you can serve up a moveable feast of chairs, tables, cushions, planters and lanterns. All these should coordinate with your interior decor — become part of it, really — to encourage seasonal migration from house to garden and back. A happy transition, indeed.

CHAPTER SIX

GARDEN ELEMENTS

*Garden elements —
fountains, pools, sculpture, furniture,
containers, statuary and lighting —
are an integral part of the design scheme.
As architecture, ornament, flight of
fancy or form of self-expression,
they are among the gardener's most
pleasant responsibilities.*

THE MAGIC *of* WATER

*The slightest trickle of
water brings calm to
the garden and intensifies
one's sense of sanctuary.
The classic lavabo
fountain (right) echoes
the formal, architectural
character of its garden.
A small, still basin
of water (below) packs
a surprise punch of
color with a bright and
light-reflective mosaic
of fanciful fish.*

As soon as people started to make gardens, they put water in them. This was partly because the first gardens were created in hot and arid lands, where a supply of water was needed close at hand to irrigate the garden and sustain plant life — but also because water has mystical and symbolic significance as the giver of life. It is a fundamental element through which we establish oneness with nature.

Water is a natural in small gardens, but first a warning: all water gardening requires time and attention; it is not a low-maintenance option. To keep ponds and pools clean and beautiful, you must work at achieving a balanced ecosystem.

After that, good housekeeping and vigilance are necessary.

A water feature may be as big or as small as you fancy. In any form or size, it brings character and an atmosphere of calm to your space, keeping the spirit in and the noise and intrusion of the street out. Like everything else in the garden, it must play a role in the overall design — not just be tacked on as an afterthought.

❧ The slightest water feature is a wall- or fence-mounted lavabo that recirculates water in a gentle trickle. It has a small but pleasing effect suitable to a tiny garden and is virtually maintenance-free.

❧ Still pools — those with no visible water movement — are reflective, tranquil and ideal for striking plants such as water lilies, which grow best in undisturbed water. Pools with moving water — in a fountain, a cascade or spouting from statuary — add life, sound and sparkle.

❧ Strong geometric shapes are suitable for formal gardens where the pool might be raised above ground level to provide seating at the water's edge. Natural or random shapes work best in less-formal settings, where a small cascade or waterfall also seems at home.

❧ Whether you use a flexible plastic liner, a prefabricated fiberglass form or on-site poured concrete to make your pool, the most difficult task is masking the edges — the point at which the container meets the surrounding earth or structure. Nothing is more off-putting than a pond or pool showing its underwear.

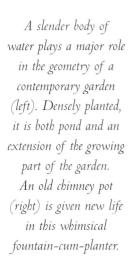

A slender body of water plays a major role in the geometry of a contemporary garden (left). Densely planted, it is both pond and an extension of the growing part of the garden. An old chimney pot (right) is given new life in this whimsical fountain-cum-planter.

Contrary to what one might expect, formal edges are easier to deal with than informal ones. Because formal shapes acknowledge human creation, they can be much more architectural. Slabs of cut stone or courses of brick make appropriate, effective and handsome copings for this kind of pond. Allow them to overhang the pond edge by a good 2 or 3 inches, so that the water seems to disappear underneath them.

Natural-looking ponds seek to suggest the complete absence of human intervention and it's difficult to achieve the soft margins one expects to see on a natural body of water. Cascades and waterfalls present the same problems. In all cases, nature does better than we can. Large pieces of stone, round river pebbles and gravel can help hide a liner but must be placed to appear as uncontrived as possible. Another approach is to gently slope one edge of the pond to form a damp area, or bog garden, for marginal planting. Such soft edges can create water-loss problems, however, as moisture is drawn through the peripheral materials (soil and planting), as by a wick, into the surrounding earth.

Waterfalls or cascades are a striking addition to a natural slope, but they should not be added to flat-as-a-pancake sites where they will scream contrivance. Waterfalls that emerge inexplicably from fences are perhaps the most egregious design folly of our times.

Walking on water is different. Bridges, boardwalks and stepping stones create wonderful opportunities to be surrounded by water and to view its reflections, plants and pond life from a different perspective. An overhanging deck can achieve the same effect.

In a small space, it's possible to make water the focal point of your design rather than just an incidental part of it. Ponds connected by bridges and boardwalks to small areas for seating and planting make a sensationally different sort of garden.

And swimming pools are definitely possible in a small garden. They can become its organizing theme and may be utterly glamorous — though, admittedly, they are a little less than lovely through the winter. Swimming-pool gardens are great for exercise and for entertaining, but be warned they will burn a hole in your pocket.

GARDEN ORNAMENTS

The right ornament in the right place does something wonderful for a garden, giving it focus and enlivening the whole space. At the heart of this successful partnership lies compatibility of mood, form, line and scale — a harmony that's easy to recognize but often difficult to analyze, much less reproduce.

Sculptures, urns, pedestals, columns, friezes and other ornaments have long been part of the art of gardening. In classical gardens, they often had religious, symbolic or memorial significance. Today, they are largely for decoration — to give pleasure to those who use the garden.

Your choice of ornament should be a matter of personal taste — big or small, traditional or modern, architectural or fantastical. Whatever your fancy, be guided by the mood and scale of your garden, and be mindful of the role the ornament will play in your design.

❧ In a small garden, one significant piece — a sculpture or an urn — may be enough. At the center of radiating paths or as a major focal point, it becomes the organizing principle of the whole space. Smaller pieces, on the other hand, might be placed around the garden as hidden surprises or to mark the turn in, or the end of, a path.

❧ While large things are needed as a focal point or to catch the eye, something small and lovely can be given more importance by placing it on a plinth or some other raised structure. Remember, though, that too modest a piece grandly displayed will seem out of place.

❧ Against the clean backdrop of a wall or hedge, an ornament takes on a bold presence. Its profile and fine detail stand out clearly and without distraction.

Traditional figurative pieces and modern sculpture both display well this way. When ornaments are set against or among flowers and foliage, their detail is less striking. Instead, it is the compatibility of their lines and color with the background that is engaging and exciting.

❧ Echoing shapes can also be effective. A pointed obelisk looks monumental set alone in open space. But, partnered with other similar shapes (perhaps clipped evergreens) and emerging from soft planting at its base, it looks quite different.

❧ Walls and fences extend the decorative potential of a small space. Plant-filled containers, masks, friezes and candle sconces are charming additions to any vertical surface, but place them with care so they work with the lines of your plan. To make small hanging things more important and to integrate them into your design, try framing them with raised panels, deep mouldings or architecturally pruned planting. For a bolder look, you might set hanging ornaments in a strong, rhythmic pattern rather than in a soft, random arrangement.

❧ Bird houses and bird feeders can be highly ornamental or just plain fun. In any style and in all colors, they enliven the garden summer and winter — not least, for the multitude of birds they attract.

❧ Gardeners on a tight budget should not despair. A garden ornament does not have to be expensive, or cost anything at all. *Objets trouvés* (found objects), architectural remnants and materials taken from nature — bent twigs, bundled reeds or grasses, great wreaths of red osier dogwood — all bring the required zest to your design and express your spirit in this place.

Garden ornaments allow ample opportunity for flights of fancy — as this striking ceramic-and-copper frieze (right) proves. Bold, bright and beautiful, it reflects the owner's personality and sense of fun.

CONTAINER GARDENING

Containers are a perfect decoration for the small garden. Available in every conceivable size, shape and design, and at prices ranging from top of the line to almost nothing, they can be an important sculptural element or simply an extra opportunity for planting.

❧ Small containers can be planted with abandon and grouped together in an ever-changing tableau. They are the garden's moveable feast. Use them to play and experiment with new plants and plant combinations, or place them strategically as part of the garden's architecture — atop a stone pier, to decorate the crest of a wall or stacked one after another up a flight of steps.

❧ Hanging planters are a great way to extend the limits of a small space. Window boxes, hanging baskets, wall- or fence-mounted pots and planter bags make it possible to lift plants out of the shade into whatever limited sunshine your garden enjoys.

❧ There are as many ways of planting a container as there are gardeners to plant them. It's a matter of personal style and of what you want to grow. In a formal garden, or as a counterpoint to a busy planting scheme, containers of architectural evergreens are very effective — clipped box or yew, perhaps combined with ivy. It might be more interesting to plant around the base of a really lovely container, keeping the top empty and clearly visible. If you do plant an ornate container, keep things uncomplicated to allow the vessel to speak for itself.

In very small gardens where there is limited opportunity for ground planting, you might use flowering shrubs, roses and perennials in containers, either alone or in combination. As the plants peak, they can be moved to a prominent spot in the garden, to be replaced with other containers as they fade. Shrubs and perennials will survive the winter in large, well-insulated containers, or they can be put in the ground to overwinter, ready for repotting in the spring.

Annuals and tender perennials can be changed spring, summer and fall in endless variety. The plants for each container should be selected as you would flowers for a vase, with internal consonance and in harmony with the surrounding garden. Think of foliage as well as flowers, with plants such as German ivy and the grey-leafed licorice plant (*Helichrysum*). Small, woody plants add body to a large container.

For deep winter, evergreen boughs, twigs, spent flowerheads — even tiny lights — brighten the containers you see every day close to a main door or in full view from an important window.

The aspiring vegetable gardener can have fun with containers, too. Tomatoes, salad greens and many other vegetables, herbs and strawberries do well in the right conditions and add to the harvest table. Many edible plants are ornamental and combine well with flowering annuals. Indeed, some annuals, such as nasturtiums and pansies, have edible flowers that add color and interest to a summer salad. When fruit and vegetables are grown in containers close to a wall or fence, they should be turned from time to time for all-round exposure to the sun.

Container plants are only as good as the medium they grow in and the care they receive. Each year, use fresh,

Large, ornamental urns and jars can be lovely enough to stand alone. In a garden of lush and varied planting, their simple form calms the whole scene and adds an air of tranquility.

rich topsoil and a dose of organic fertilizer. Water well when you first plant them and keep them moist — not wet, not dry — throughout the growing season. All pots must have drainage holes to allow excess water to escape. Feed container plants frequently for a good bloom or harvest, since nutrients quickly leach from the soil as water drains through the pots. Deadhead and pinch back frequently.

GARDEN FURNISHINGS

Many garden furnishings are pleasing ornaments — and many ornaments are elegant furniture. Certainly, a handsome bench or garden seat of teak, cast or wrought iron, bent wire or stone makes as effective a focal point as any statue.

❧ Place such pieces so they can be used conveniently, either close to the house or deep in the garden for a leisurely pause. Treat them as objects of beauty. Surround them with low, spilling plants such as thyme, catmint and lavender that release their perfume when bruised, or frame them formally with clipped hedging.

❧ Seating walls, built-in benches (perhaps over a storage locker) and turf seats that use growing grass or herbs as a cushion add to the repertoire of permanent outdoor furniture. Benches built around the trunk of a tree are also an excellent application for a small garden where anything that is three-in-one is a good idea — here, a tree, a seat and an ornament.

❧ Outdoor dining tables and chairs, loungers and daybeds are more functional, it's true, but they should also be chosen with the same care you'd accord indoor furnishings. Coordinating the shape, color and style of outdoor and indoor furnishings enhances the connection between the two spaces. In fact, some furniture may be suitable in both settings.

❧ Small folding pieces, such as French café chairs, are a useful addition to any household. They look charming in the garden and expand your seating capacity for large family gatherings inside the house.

❧ Color is an important part of any furnishings. Natural hues always work, but sometimes a splash of color that picks up other tones in the garden can also look sensational — perhaps a white bench, surrounded with white 'Mount Hood' daffodils and set under a white flowering crab apple tree. Color might be on pieces of painted furniture, or cushions added when the garden is in use.

A blanket of snow transforms summer furniture into winter sculpture, extending the seasonal appeal of the garden.

GARDEN LIGHTING

Small gardens seem made for use at night. Because they're an extension of the house, we naturally spill into them in the evening for some quiet time or to entertain friends. Garden lighting makes this both a practical possibility and a beautiful experience.

❧ Ambient, or all-round, lighting softly reveals whole areas of the garden that would otherwise be totally black, but it's a difficult effect to execute because the light source, which must be set up high, tends to catch and dazzle the eye. To some extent, this problem can be countered by adding baffles to the fixtures and aiming the lights away from major vantage points.

The garden after dark can be a magical place. Lighting from below washes over the columns of an elegant gazebo; leaves and branches cast enchanting shadows onto the fence behind.

❧ Spotlighting structures and plants can be spectacular. Uplighting illuminates trunks, branch structure and leaves; downlighting casts shadows that dapple the space below. Backlighting throws up silhouettes; frontlighting shows the detail of form and foliage. All these are effective, both winter and summer, in making the night garden more interesting.

❧ Many garden lighting fixtures are now widely available (from specialty lighting stores and better garden centers) in the low-voltage range (12 V). They need a transformer, but are easy to install and to move around — which is a help to the amateur lighting designer who might not get it right the first time. Both regular and low-voltage lights can be controlled on a timer or with switching devices for separate parts of the garden, which makes for great flexibility. For more elaborate lighting, you may need to consult a professional.

❧ For the low-tech gardener, there is always the light of a burning flame. Candles, torches and flambeaux are a romantic way of lighting your garden and are especially right for festive occasions.

❧ Security and safety lighting are a little different and more functional. Lights over frequently used paths, steps, gates and entrances into the house or garage make the garden usable and safe at night. Security lighting intended to deter intruders is best triggered by a motion detector, rather than being left on constantly with an intrusive glare.

CHAPTER SEVEN

PLANTS
for the
SMALL
GARDEN

*Because
space is tight and often
awkward in small gardens, it's
crucial that you use your planting
opportunities well — that each
thing you choose occupies its
allotted space perfectly and carries
through the intentions of
your design.*

BEFORE *you* PLANT

Before we're seduced by fleeting blooms or intoxicating perfume, we should examine plants with the clear eye of an architect. The great American landscape designer Fletcher Steele (1885-1917) was taken with the French approach to horticulture. "A tree to them is not good in itself," he wrote, "but for what can be done with it, as with brick or a thousand gallons of water." Steele encourages us to identify each plant's form and inherent character — its size, shape, density, texture and quality of color — so we can understand how best to use it.

Plants for small gardens must earn their keep with a combination of appealing qualities — form, foliage, flowers, fruit and fragrance — so that, summer or winter, there is always something interesting to see. Look for plants that please in more than one way, for more than one brief season, and group them in a sequence of effects, from spring bloom to late fall color and winter form.

Copying nature's way of planting in layers, or distinct canopies, helps us make good use of our limited three-dimensional space and find the right plant for any given spot, even the tightest corner. Starting at the top with large trees, through smaller trees and shrubs, finally coming down to earth with perennials and ground covers, we can stack the different layers of planting so that each has room to grow without crowding the garden or its neighbors, and our scheme reads as a carefully orchestrated whole.

Getting to know your plants is essential to the making of a garden. Fortunately, it is also one of its most pleasurable tasks. Botanical gardens, garden centers, other people's gardens and good plant manuals will supply the information you need. Look carefully, think

four seasons and remember that young, container-grown plants can look very different at maturity; notes in the garden-center catalogues about final size are to be heeded. Resist, if you can, the urge to acquire every wonderful thing you see; buy only when you're sure a plant fits your needs perfectly.

The cultural requirements of a plant must be part of your thinking, too. Placing sun-lovers in a shady spot or shade-lovers in the sun will inevitably result in disappointment. Be sure you understand, and cater to, the growing needs of each thing you decide to plant — from light conditions and moisture, to the pH and character of the soil — and be prepared to tinker and fine-tune, for plants, like people, can be a little unpredictable.

Use your scaled base plan (see Chapter One) to block in plants as abstract forms, working from the largest, which provide the framework, to the smallest, which add bulk and fine detail. Each plant should have a role in relation to the house and the built parts of the garden — as well as to other plants — in a well-balanced composition of shapes and sizes, masses and voids, dark and light. Make your specific choices only at the end, staying firmly within the parameters you've set.

To help you visualize how larger plants, such as trees, shrubs or a hedge, might look in your landscape, try sketching them onto an enlarged image of the garden. From a major vantage, take a series of photographs and tape them together to form a panoramic view. Enlarge the whole image in photocopies and sketch in each plant at its mature size — either on an overlay of tracing paper or in felt tip pen directly onto the copy. Trial and error with pen and paper are less exacting than with shovel and spade.

THE 5-F FORMULA *for* SUCCESSFUL PLANTING

Good planting design combines form and function and puts the right plant in the right place. It brings together different shapes, textures and colors, as images on an everchanging canvas. The 5-F Formula helps you to consider the qualities of each plant and to assess its possible role in your garden scheme. Plants that satisfy on three or more of these counts are right for small gardens, where everything must play its part and earn its keep.

FORM
❧ size, shape, density, character of branches and twigs

FOLIAGE
❧ evergreen or deciduous; size and shape; fine or coarse texture; shiny or matte; spring, summer and fall color

FLOWERS
❧ color, size and shape; period and length of bloom; appearance after blooming

FRUIT
❧ size, form and color; edible and attractive to birds; persistent through winter; messy

FRAGRANCE
❧ type, period and duration; source (from flowers high up or close to the ground)

TREES

In a small garden, you may feel you need one or two substantial trees to lend weight, balance and scale to your scheme. Look for varieties that don't branch too close to the ground, with an open, airy canopy that lends a sense of enclosure while allowing light to filter through to the layers of planting below.

Where you need privacy from on high — perhaps from a neighbor's upper deck — it's better to use trees with a feathery canopy as a somewhat translucent screen, than something denser that will make the garden seem closed in and dark. And be warned: while many columnar trees, such as the columnar forms of oak and maple, look like a great option for tall privacy screens, they are not for very tiny gardens because they eventually develop a wide, low girth of 12 to 15 feet (4 to 5 m).

❧ Honey locust (*Gleditsia triacanthos*, in variety, Zone 4), with its graceful rounded head and fern-like foliage, casts light dappled shade. At maturity, it reaches a height of more than 30 feet (10 m). Locusts leaf out late and

*Clockwise from top left:
Honey Locust
(Gleditsia triacanthos)
in autumn; Paperback
Maple (Acer griseum)
with autumn leaves and
bark; Mountain Ash
(Sorbus aucuparia)
in winter.*

these medium-size trees appear as a great cloud of white blossoms; through the summer, they bear dark, glossy leaves; in autumn, their foliage, which lasts well into early winter, turns a stunning red, orange and yellow. *P. calleryana* 'Bradford' has a rounded canopy and can reach 40 feet (13 m) at maturity, whereas 'Capital' is more slender and upright, reaching a maximum height of 36 feet (12 m), with a spread of up to 13 feet (4 m).

❧ The ivory silk tree lilac (*Syringa reticulata* 'Ivory Silk', Zone 2) is a tougher customer. Sturdy and compact, with a mature height of 25 feet (8 m), it never fails to thrill with a show of creamy white flowers in early July, when most flowering trees have finished their annual display.

❧ The bird cherry tree (*Prunus padus* 'Colorata', Zone 2) grows to 30 feet (10 m) and has maroon foliage and pink flowers. Its sister, mayday cherry (*Prunus padus* var. 'Dropmore', Zone 3),

drop their leaves early, allowing sunlight to flood into the garden during the cooler months of spring and fall. Mountain ash (*Sorbus aucuparia*, in variety, Zone 3) grows more than 25 feet (8 m) tall and combines an elegant, symmetrical form with early-summer blossom and bright red fruit in fall. Both are good choices for the small garden. Native ironwood (*Ostrya virginiana*, Zone 4) is another attractive possibility. With rough bark and fine twigs that bear dark nutlets and catkins, this handsome tree tolerates both sun and shade. Its mature height is 32 feet (10.6 m).

❧ Ornamental pears (*Pyrus calleryana*, Zone 5) have potential for small gardens in warmer areas. In May,

is of similar height and produces large chains of white, fragrant flowers and dark green leaves that turn bronze in fall. Both are excellent candidates for gardens that know the meaning of winter in Canada.

❧ More unusual is the paperbark maple (*Acer griseum*, Zone 6), with its relatively small, fine leaves that color dramatically in fall and its exquisite, cinnamon-colored exfoliating bark. "Verbal descriptions cannot do justice to this ornamental asset, and only after one has been privileged to view the bark firsthand can one fully appreciate the character," says Michael Dirr in his bible, *Manual of Woody Landscape Plants.* It grows to a height of more than 20 feet (7 m).

This chapter gives suggestions for plants that are particularly suited to the small garden — from trees to ground covers. Trees and shrubs are given special attention because, for limited spaces, they must be chosen with considerable care. Vines are also highlighted as they are exceptionally valuable small-space plants. As perennials and bulbs are less garden-specific — in the right space and growing conditions, most are acceptable — our suggestions are limited to a few diminutive gems without which a small garden is hardly complete.

(Above) 'Red Jade' Crab Apple (Malus 'Red Jade'); (right) Standard of Dwarf Lilac (Syringa meyeri 'Palibin').

❧ The much reviled, though aptly named, tree of heaven (*Ailanthus altissima*, Zone 4) has its place, too, because it seems to grow anywhere, even in a scratch of earth at the side of a road. It has a pleasant, high and light canopy that reaches up to 50 feet (16 m) — a little less, in tight urban settings — compound leaves and spectacular clusters of winged fruit that are dazzling in late summer and stay on the branches to make an eerie rustling sound as they blow in the winter wind.

❧ Mid-size trees (approximately 15 feet/5 m tall) may be all you need if you have large trees in the landscape around you. Suitable members of the *Prunus* family include 'Newport' flowering plum (*P. ceracifera* 'Newport',

Zone 4), with pale pink flowers, dark purple leaves and fruit; and the weeping Japanese cherry (*P. serrulata* 'Kiku Shidare', Zone 6) that bears deep pink, double flowers on pendulous branches.

❧ Crab apples are also an excellent choice, especially those that hold their fruit over the winter — such as *Malus* 'Donald Wyman' (Zone 4), *M.* 'White Angel' (Zone 4) and the weeping 'Red Jade' (Zone 3). There is a truly slender crab apple, *M. baccata* 'Columnaris' (Zone 2) that, although taller (24 feet/8 m), develops a maximum girth of about 6 feet (2 m) and carries its yellow fruit well into the winter.

❧ Some trees that start life as a shrub and are either

pruned up to a tree-like form or grafted onto a taller stem may be right for your small garden. Serviceberries — *Amelanchier canadensis* and *A. canadensis* 'Ballerina' (both Zone 4) and the hardier Saskatoon berry, *A. alnifolia* (Zone 1) — are delightful small shrubs/trees that tolerate shade. They blossom in a cloud of white early in spring, bear edible fruit that attracts birds (and humans) and have wonderful fall color. What more could one ask?

❦ Another Canadian native, the redbud (*Cercis canadensis*, Zone 6) is a highly recommended early-spring bloomer, elegant of form and foliage and tolerant of shade. Growing to a maximum height of 12 feet (4 m), it's covered with tiny pea-like mauve-pink flowers in spring before the leaves appear.

❦ Standards of hydrangea (*H. paniculata* 'Grandiflora', Zone 3b), with late-summer blooms; dwarf lilac (*Syringa*

Devil's-walkingstick (*Aralia spinosa*, Zone 5), of similar height, rounds out the trio in spiny fashion. This might not be your choice if you have children or if you must brush closely by its prickly stems. However, this large shrub is a novelty in the small garden, bearing its large leaves and great clusters of late flowers and fruit high on club-like stems.

SHRUBS

Small and medium-size shrubs form the middle layer of the canopy. Their architectural quality is especially important because they are at eye level; they're the ones we walk and sit among, the ones that fill out the garden's usable space.

Before you buy, decide what role these mid-size plants are to play on the botanical stage of your garden. Do you need dense shrubs with sturdy, non-reflective leaves to create a strong barrier? Something bold and upright to act as a focal point? Or perhaps a light, transparent form to softly divide two spaces? As always, think in broad, abstract terms before you make specific choices and

---

A WORD *on* PLANTING NEW TREES

If you have a small lot in a new, treeless subdivision, consider getting together with your neighbors to plant one serious, large specimen tree, such as an oak or maple, for every three or four lots. Large trees are the best thing for making a new place feel settled — and even if you've moved on before you can reap the benefits of your planning, others will enjoy the fruits of your planting.

---

meyeri 'Palibin', Zone 3), that bears highly perfumed mauve flowers in early summer; and euonymus (*E. fortunei*, in variety, Zones 4 to 5b), a broad-leafed evergreen with plain or variegated foliage, all stay at about eye level with appropriate pruning, although they do develop more heft than their modest forms suggest when you first purchase them.

❦ Lilac, sumac and devil's-walkingstick grow, or can be pruned to be, tall and skinny enough of branch to fit into a tight corner whence their foliage arches outward. Lilac (*Syringa*, Zone 2+) of any sort is irresistible in bloom — what greater delight than cutting a sweetly scented armful? — but not very interesting otherwise. Plant lilacs in your small garden only if you adore them and can't imagine a garden without them. Staghorn and cutleaf sumacs (*Rhus typhina* and *R. typhina* 'Lacinata', Zone 3), which grow to 10 feet (2.5 m), have no showy blossom but great structure and foliage, with brilliant fall color and prominent crimson, pyramid-shape fruit.

be sure you choose plants that are suited to the growing conditions in your garden.

There are many wonderful shrubs available in the ever-expanding Canadian marketplace. Your difficulty will be not in finding something suitable, but in resisting the urge to buy many more than you need. Here are some sure-fire suggestions.

❦ **Large shrubs** with great form and a degree of heft are ideal as specimens — perhaps as the centerpiece of a small paved courtyard garden, to fill a generous corner or to separate spaces. Many of the Japanese maples are perfect for small gardens. The 'Inaba Shidare' maple (*Acer palmatum* 'Dissectum Inaba Shidare', Zone 5b), with deeply cut red foliage, and the Japanese purple maple (*A. palmatum* 'Atropurpureum', Zone 6), are among the larger choices, with a mature height of 15 to 18 feet (5 to 6 m); the green cutleaf maple (*A. palmatum* 'Dissectum Viride', Zone 6) is smaller, with a height of about 6 feet (2 m).

❧ Sea buckthorn (*Hippophae rhamnoides*, Zone 3), at 8 feet (2.5 m) tall with slender, grey leaves and bright orange winter fruit, is an interesting and very hardy choice for colder regions — but only the female bears fruit and she needs a mate somewhere nearby for pollination.

❧ Some of the smaller magnolia are great, too. 'Betty' (*M. liliiflora* 'Betty', Zone 5), with its reddish-purple flowers, grows to a height of less than 10 feet (3 m); the small star magnolia, 'King Rose' (*M. stellata* 'King Rose', Zone 4), with showy pink blooms, reaches a height of 5 feet (1.5 m).

❧ Chinese flowering dogwoods (*Cornus kousa chinensis*, Zone 4) merit mention for their creamy white, flower-like bracts that sparkle on horizontal branches for up to 6 weeks from early June, often taking on a pinkish hue as they mature. Though flowering dogwoods grow to around 20 feet (7 m), the lower branches can be removed as the shrub matures to form a small tree-like specimen that floats over other plantings.

❧ **Many medium-size shrubs** (5 to 7 feet/ 1.5 to 2.3 m) are suitable for the back of a small perennial border or the center of freestanding flower beds. Viburnums offer a range of possibilities — from the Korean spice bush (*V. carlesi*, Zone 4), with its intoxicating pink/white blooms in early spring, through Maries doublefile (*V. plicatum* 'Mariesii', Zone 5) that presents large, flat white blooms on very horizontal branches in mid-summer, and the summer snowflake (*V. plicatum* 'Summer Snowflake', Zone 6) that offers a compact form and flowers from spring to late summer.

❧ Butterfly bush (*Buddleia davidii*, Zone 5), which really does attract butterflies, is fun placed to poke out, up and over smaller shrubs or perennial masses. As it flowers on new wood, which it produces at lightning speed, it can be cut down to the ground each spring to limit the size and density of its branches.

❧ Of similar stature are hydrangeas of all sorts — from peegee (*H. paniculata* 'Grandiflora', Zone 3b), which grows to 9 feet (3 m), and the smaller oak-leafed (*H. quercifolia*, Zone 5), both with white flowers, to the lacecap varieties (Zone 6) in blue and pink. Hydrangeas are excellent value for their late (some, very late) bloom and the fact that the dried flowers persist long into the winter. White hydrangeas combine well with the sparkling white/green variegated leaves of the silverleaf dogwood (*Cornus alba* 'Elegantissima', Zone 2), which might be taken for summer-long bloom. The dogwood also boasts bright red twigs in winter.

❧ Gardeners in the coldest parts of Canada should not lose heart — the choices are still myriad. Try the dwarf lilac (*Syringa meyeri* 'Palibin', Zone 3) that grows 4 feet (1.2 m) tall and has small, well-formed leaves and highly scented mauve flowers; the dwarf burning bush (*Euonymus alatus* 'Compactus', Zone 3), of similar height, that comes into its own later in the year with flamboyant foliage, scarlet fruit and strange winged branches; the very hardy and attractive dwarf American cranberry (*Viburnum trilobum* 'Compactum', Zone 2), 5 feet (1.5 m) high, that carries handsome, flat-topped white blooms in late May and bright red fruit that persists from September to December (when the birds get hungry); and false spirea (*Sorbaria sorbifolia*, Zone 2), with its attractive cut foliage and cream flower plumes in July that stay intact to provide interest through the winter. The false spirea needs discipline but, at 6 feet (2 m) tall, is a lovely option to fill a corner where it can be contained.

❧ **The smallest shrubs** mix well with perennials. Their scale is right and they add a degree of woody structure to plantings that otherwise disappear in winter. It's certainly possible to use small shrubs as a substitute for perennials. In combination with vines and a few good trees, they make a fine planting scheme.

Clockwise from top: Dwarf Burning Bush (Euonymus alatus *'Compactus'*); *Lacecap Hydrangea* (H. macrophylla); *Butterfly Bush* (Buddleia davidii).

❧ Note that the words *nana* or *compacta* in a plant's botanical name denote smallness of stature — as in *Euonymus alatus* 'Compactus' (the dwarf burning bush). Upright or mounded, feathery or cascading, there are many stellar performers in this group.

❧ Daphne is a must for the partly shady garden, particularly *D. X burkwoodii* 'Carol Mackie' (Zone 4). It grows to 3 feet (1 m) and has tiny green/cream variegated leaves and sensationally perfumed spring blooms.

❧ Variegated kerria (*K. japonica* 'Picta', Zone 5), of similar height, is another shade-tolerant jewel for the spring garden. With yellow buttercup-like flowers that recur occasionally throughout the year and delicate white/green variegated leaves borne on bright green stems, it is truly a four-season plant.

❧ For sunnier spots, there's a multitude of small (2 to 3 feet/60 to 90 cm), good-looking spireas. From *Spiraea X bumalda* 'Crispa' (Zone 3), with bright pink flowers and deeply cleft, wrinkly leaves, to *S. japonica* 'Shirobana' (Zone 3) that boasts both pale pink and white flowers on a single plant. Both bear their spent flowerheads in skeleton form through the winter.

❧ Yellow cinquefoils (*Potentilla fruticosa*, Zone 2) are familiar to most gardeners but they are also available in white ('Mount Everest' and 'Abbottswood'), pink ('Pink Queen') and flame ('Red Ace'). With their compact form and fine foliage, long-flowering cinquefoils are pleasing, trouble-free plants.

❧ Some diminutive (18 to 20 inches/45 to 50 cm) shrubs, such as cotoneaster (technically, a broadleaf evergreen, but not very evergreen in harsh climates), make a good ground cover. *C. dammeri* 'Coral Beauty' (Zone 4) and the rock spray (*C. horizontalis*, Zone 5) have an attractive twiggy form, delicate flowers and showy red berries. Cutleaf stephanandra is on the same scale (*S. incisa* 'Crispa', Zone 4) but of softer habit. It cascades over retaining walls, with fine foliage that turns mellow yellow in the fall.

Choosing and siting the right shrubs is only the beginning, of course. For all plants to do well, you must learn their foibles and cater to their needs. Read up on when you should prune to guarantee blooms every year, how to feed and water, what pests and diseases to look out for. Freshly planted material needs time to settle into its new home, so be patient. Note, too, that as shrubs grow and develop into their mature form, they will change and play a different role in the garden scheme. At first, they are squat and tight to the ground; as they mature, they expose the space below them, which can then be planted with low perennials and ground covers. Nor is it total heresy to remove a shrub if it grows too big. Planned obsolescence in the garden becomes part of the natural process when branches, twigs and leaves are mulched and returned to the soil.

EVERGREENS

Plants that stay green through the winter are a definite asset in the Canadian garden — and if they have wonderful form and beautiful blooms, so much the better. Evergreens generally read dark and dense and should be balanced equally throughout the garden, particularly as they become more dominant in winter.

❧ In milder regions, broadleaf evergreens such as box (either closely clipped or grown as an open specimen), euonymus and holly add greatly to the structure of a planting scheme. All keep their color well and don't look too sad by the end of a long, cold winter.

❧ Acid-loving shrubs such as rhododendron, mountain laurel (*Kalmia latifolia*, Zone 6), azaleas and Japanese pieris (*P. japonica*, Zone 5b) add bloom to the palette, although they are tender and they definitely need the right soil (4 to 6 pH) to thrive. Small-leaved rhododendrons such as 'P.J.M.', 'Olga Mezitt' and the dwarf 'Ramapo' (all Zone 4) are good hardy choices, as pleasing for their foliage as for their bloom.

❧ Firethorn (*Pyracantha*) is an attractive shrub for the small garden. With its small evergreen leaves, white summer flowers and striking red or orange berries that last well into winter, it can either be grown as a shrub or trained up a wall or fence. 'Yukon Belle' (*P. coccinea* 'Yukon Belle', Zone 4), which bears orange fruit, is hardier than other varieties.

❧ Needle-bearing evergreens are also effective players in the small-garden planting scheme, but be careful not to choose specimens that will grow too big. Many of the low, almost creeping, junipers — such as dwarf Japanese juniper (*Juniperus procumbens* 'Nana',

THE CARE *and* FEEDING *of your* GARDEN

Small-space gardens need as much, if not more, care and attention as large gardens. Pruning, staking, tying back and dead-heading are all the more important because every detail shows and counts in intimate spaces. In other words, small gardens can quickly look messy.

❧ Looking after the things that don't show matters, too. Pest and disease control through careful gardening practice and early intervention, fertilizing and feeding are of utmost importance. So is the task of preparing and maintaining your soil. Great plants grow from well-tended earth, so start off well and keep enriching and enlivening your soil with organic mulches, preferably from your own composter.

❧ Careful tending of your private domain will bring both garden and gardener a little closer to heaven.

Zone 4), tamarix (*J. sabina* 'Tamarisifolia', Zone 2) and Arcadia (*J. sabina* 'Arcadia', Zone 2) — bring interesting form and foliage color to a sunny spot.

❧ Dwarf mugho pines (*Pinus mugo* 'Pumilio', Zone 1) are compact and pleasingly vertical in habit, whereas dwarf hemlocks (*Tsuga canadensis*) are much softer and woodsy looking — 'Hussii' is upright and irregular, 'Nana Gracilis' displays more drooping and graceful form, while 'Cole's Prostrata' is slow-growing, very low and weeping (all three are hardy to Zone 4). Dwarf hemlocks are among the few conifers that tolerate shade.

❧ The dwarf Alberta spruce (*Picea glauca* 'Conica') and its sister, 'Alberta Globe' (both Zone 4), with fine grass-green, very dense foliage, are interesting and slow-growing specimens for a small space. Dwarf forms of cedar (*Thuja occidentalis*) are also worth consideration. 'Holmstrop' (Zone 3) is a pyramidal form with bright green foliage; 'Sunkist' (Zone 2) is another pyramid, this time with golden yellow foliage; while 'Little Giant' (Zone 3) has a globular form and dark green foliage. Topiaried evergreens — spruce, cedar, box and yew — fit neatly into small planting schemes where their bold architectural shapes add both form and character.

❧ Most full-size conifers (except those, such as cedar and yew, that can be clipped), are not a great choice for small gardens because they grow too big. Severe pruning to limit their size only results in sad and distorted specimens. When choosing evergreens for your garden, make sure they are the dwarf form that will fit comfortably in your limited space.

*Hall's honeysuckle (*Lonicera japonica* 'Halliana') with abutilon.*

VINES

Climbing, twining or creeping, vines are surely the quintessential plants for a small garden. Generously clothing walls, fences, screens and structures, they help compensate for limited in-ground planting. Some add permanent form and scale; others, such as the larger flowering clematis, are spectacular but more ephemeral.

❧ You might choose planes of luscious green, such as the broadleaf evergreen *Euonymus fortunei* 'Sarcoxie' (Zone 5) that, in milder situations, will climb to second-floor windows; or deciduous ivies such as Virginia creeper (*Parthenocissus quinquefolia*, Zone 2b), Engleman's ivy (*P. quinquefolia* 'Englemanii', Zone 2b) or Boston ivy (*P. tricupidata* 'Veitchii', Zone 4). All make fast work of covering a large area, have striking fall color and present an interesting tracery of branches for winter interest.

❧ Large flowering vines add tremendous stature to even the smallest garden. None is more spectacular then the climbing hydrangea (*Hydrangea anomala petiolaris*, Zone 4),

Wisteria with alliums and viburnum.

which grows to 20 feet (7 m) and has white flowers in early summer that become delicate clusters of cinnamon-brown in winter on sturdy exfoliating branches. Nor is wisteria (*W. floribunda* or *W. sinensis*, Zone 4) a common beauty. Twisting and twining over any garden structure, or trained over wires espalier-like on a wall or fence, its blooms of white, pink, mauve or purple are scented and truly breathtaking. In winter, its eccentric form bears frost and snow and casts eerie shadows from the low winter sun.

❧ Species clematis, such as the spring-flowering alpine (*C. alpina*, Zone 2) and late-summer-flowering virgin's bower (*C. virginiana*, Zone 4), may be less familiar than the large-flowering varieties, but they are excellent value in the small garden. Sweet autumn clematis (*C. paniculata*, Zone 5), with scented white flowers in late August, and the very hardy 'Prairie Traveller's Joy' (Zone 1), also with white flowers, are large, rampant vines that are effective for massive cover. Because they produce flowers on old wood, these clematis don't need radical pruning every year. They just get bigger and better and more beautiful as they age. With attractive foliage and, in many cases, feathery, persistent seed heads, they are an excellent choice.

❧ Honeysuckle, both the orange/red flowering 'Dropmore Scarlet' (*Lonicera* x *brownii* 'Dropmore Scarlet', Zone 3) and Hall's (*L. japonica* 'Halliana', Zone 5), with fragrant cream/yellow flowers; bittersweet (*Celastrus sandens*, Zone 3b) that displays trusses of bright orange-red berries late into winter; and Dutchman's pipe (*Aristolochia durior*, Zone 5), with heart-shape foliage and strange pipe-shape blooms, are all suitable, interesting and beautiful choices for the small garden.

With such an array of hardy vines at your disposal, it should be possible to make an art of vertical planting. As always, choose specimens that do double- or triple-duty with form, flowers and foliage.

PERENNIALS

As the scale of your planting moves from shrubs down to perennials and ground covers, continue to think of each plant's architectural qualities. Some are soft and round, others more bold and upright. Mix the shapes and forms to enhance the built parts of your garden. A vertical plant, for example, strengthens upright elements such as gate posts, columns or sculpture.

Leaf quality is particularly important in small gardens. Establish a theme by associating leaves that are in some ways similar and in some ways different — perhaps tall, spiky leaves with flatter, round ones of similar hue. This technique avoids visual confusion and allows each specimen to enliven its companions. Look for plants that keep good foliage through the season, and strive for a sequence of bloom from spring to fall. Limit your palette to a few good choices rather than a multitude of different plants. Any beloved perennial will work in a small garden if you have space and the appropriate light for it.

❧ Ground covers and tiny plants are particularly useful because they allow you to plant a final layer close to the earth. Spring bloomers include periwinkle (*Vinca minor*, Zone 4), with shiny evergreen leaves; foamflower (*Tiarella cordifolia*, Zone 3) which blooms with fluffy white spikes and has leaves that bronze in winter; and sweet woodruff (*Galium odoratum*, Zone 4), again with attractive leaves and clusters of starry, white flowers. All these enjoy shade.

❧ In summer, perennial cranesbill (*Geranium*) are a must in small spaces. In many different varieties and colors from white and pale pink to magenta and blue, there is

Species Tulip

Snowdrops (Galanthus) *are the harbingers of spring.*

one that's right for any spot. Look for the diminutive
G. cinereum 'Ballerina' (Zone 5), with purple-pink, darkly
veined flowers; *G. dalmaticum* (Zone 3), with shell-pink
flowers on a glossy green cushion of leaves that turn red
in fall; and the larger, shade-tolerant *G. macrorrhizum*, with
blooms in various shades of pink and aromatic leaves
that are evergreen in mild conditions.

In dry, sunny locations, saxifrages fit the bill, especially
S. paniculata, with its clusters of grey-green rosettes held
tight to the ground. Low speedwells (e.g., *Veronica prostrata*,
Zone 5) and thymes (e.g., *Thymus praecox*, Zone 2) creep
delightfully between and over paving stones. Try the
many forms of hen and chickens (*Sempervivum*, Zone 1)
and dwarf stonecrops (*Sedum*, Zone 2); both flower
attractively but are most remarkable for their succulent
foliage.

For late summer, look to the smaller astilbes (e.g.,
A. chinensis 'Pumila', Zone 3), with flower spikes that last
well into winter; to compact hybrid asters such as
'Audrey', that flowers mauve-blue, and 'Nesthakchen'
(Zone 3), with clear pink blooms; and to members of
the heuchera family such as *H. micrantha* 'Palace Purple',
'Bressingham Bronze' (Zone 4) with sensational deep-
purple, ruffled foliage, and 'Northern Fire' (Zone 2),
with green, white-marked leaves.

BULBS

Few gardeners would consider their heaven complete
without spring- and summer-flowering bulbs. After a
long winter, their arrival is certainly one of the high
points of the gardening calendar.

Bulbs of all sorts and sizes are right for the small
garden because they take up comparatively little space. In
bloom, they poke up through other plants among whose
foliage their fading leaves will be neatly hidden.

Snowdrops (*Galanthus*, Zone 4) are the harbingers of
spring, sometimes even blooming in the snow. Species tulips
come next — *tarda, bakeri* 'Lilac Wonder' et al — and then
the multitude of mid-season daffodils. *Narcissus* 'Thalia',
'Jacksnipe' and 'Trevithian' are attractive dwarf varieties; they
look enchanting planted with grape hyacinths (*Muscari*,
Zone 3) that bloom at the same time. Lily-flowered and
Darwin tulips flower toward the end of the spring bulb
flush; strong and upright, both come in a dazzling array of
colors to complement any planting scheme.

Wild hyacinth (*Camassia*, Zone 4) and summer
snowflake (*Leucojum aestivum*, Zone 4) usher in the summer-
flowering bulbs — alliums and lilies in all their profuse
color and scent. As soon as the summer bulbs are finished,
it's time to start thinking about what to add next spring.

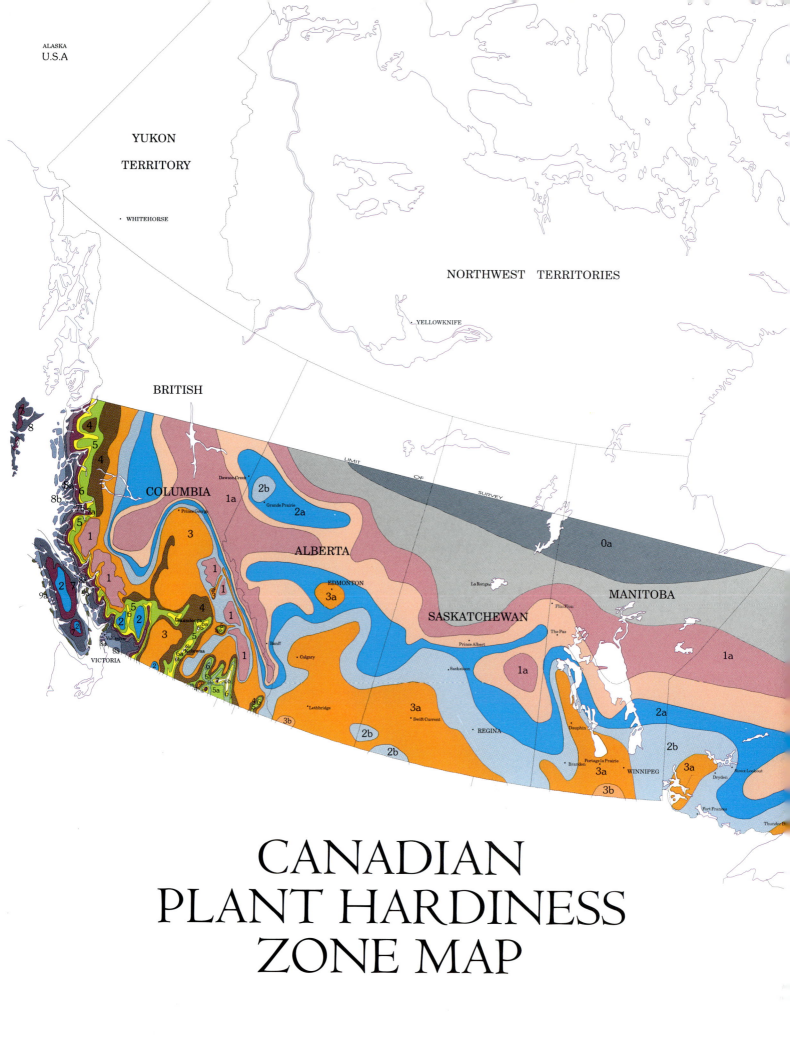

CANADIAN
PLANT HARDINESS
ZONE MAP

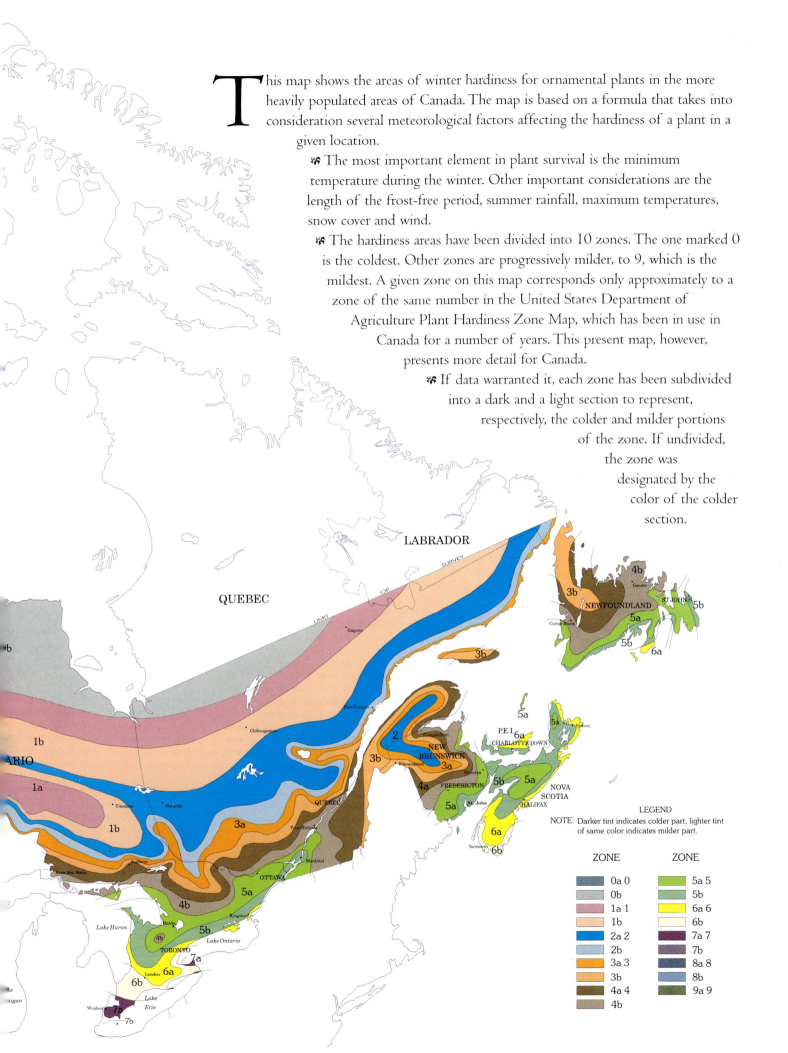

This map shows the areas of winter hardiness for ornamental plants in the more heavily populated areas of Canada. The map is based on a formula that takes into consideration several meteorological factors affecting the hardiness of a plant in a given location.

❧ The most important element in plant survival is the minimum temperature during the winter. Other important considerations are the length of the frost-free period, summer rainfall, maximum temperatures, snow cover and wind.

❧ The hardiness areas have been divided into 10 zones. The one marked 0 is the coldest. Other zones are progressively milder, to 9, which is the mildest. A given zone on this map corresponds only approximately to a zone of the same number in the United States Department of Agriculture Plant Hardiness Zone Map, which has been in use in Canada for a number of years. This present map, however, presents more detail for Canada.

❧ If data warranted it, each zone has been subdivided into a dark and a light section to represent, respectively, the colder and milder portions of the zone. If undivided, the zone was designated by the color of the colder section.

LABRADOR

QUEBEC

NEWFOUNDLAND

ST. JOHN'S

P.E.I.
CHARLOTTETOWN

NEW
BRUNSWICK

FREDERICTON

NOVA
SCOTIA
HALIFAX

LEGEND

NOTE: Darker tint indicates colder part, lighter tint of same color indicates milder part.

ZONE	ZONE
0a 0	5a 5
0b	5b
1a 1	6a 6
1b	6b
2a 2	7a 7
2b	7b
3a 3	8a 8
3b	8b
4a 4	9a 9
4b	

THE CONTRIBUTORS

❧ PENNY ARTHURS is a widely respected garden designer and the owner of her own garden design practice, The Chelsea Gardener. A graduate of The English Gardening School at London's historic Chelsea Physic Garden (one of Britain's leading schools of garden design), she designs city and country properties in and around Toronto and across the country — many of which have been featured on garden tours. She also writes regularly on garden design for *Canadian Gardening* and other magazines, lectures and makes television appearances on the subject.

❧ LIZ PRIMEAU is the editor-in-chief of *Canadian Gardening* and host of Canadian Gardening Television on Life network. In her six years with the magazine, she has visited gardens in all parts of Canada and has heard firsthand from committed Canadian gardeners about what works — or doesn't work! — in this widely varied climate of ours. An avid and experienced gardener herself, she has also been a featured speaker at gardening conferences, trade shows and garden clubs. Liz Primeau writes regularly on gardening for *The Globe and Mail*'s Design section.

Photographers

All photographs, including the cover, are by CHRISTOPHER DEW unless otherwise indicated below.

FRED BIRD:
page 72.

JANET DAVIS:
pages 40 (left), 46, 55, 63, 67, 78, 79, 80, 83, (top and bottom left), 85, 86, 87.

ADAM GIBBS:
pages 4, 10, 11, 26, 30 (inset), 32, 47, 50, 75.

FRANK KERSHAW:
pages 22 (inset), 28.

BERT KLASSEN:
pages 3, 5 (photograph of Liz Primeau), 66, 96 (background).

MARILYNN McARA:
pages 68, 69.

JERRY SHULMAN:
page 83 (bottom right).

PADDY WALES:
pages 1, 40 (inset).

Drawing on page 15 by Gail Shillingford.

Acknowledgments

We are indebted to the many gardeners who so generously provided us with the wealth of stunning and inspirational photographs which appear throughout this book. Our thanks to Mary Butterfield, Dan Chase and Tim Cross, Janet Davis, William Hurren, Julie Lane-Gay, Audrey Litherland, Robert Macaulay, Bert and Mary Manion (design by Murray Haig), Keeyla Meadows, Bill and Reiko Meagher, Barbara Nield, Selma Landen Odon (design by Terry McGlade), Wayne Renaud, Brenda Scherbatty, Beverley Sharrock, Andrew Smith and Ruth Bothern, Joseph and Antoinette Sorbara, landscape architect Neil Turnbull, and Stuart and Pauline Webber.

❧ In some cases, it was not possible to identify gardens or their owners from the photographs of garden details which appear throughout this book, or their names have not been given to ensure privacy. We acknowledge them here and are grateful for the use of this material.

SPECIAL THANKS

❧ I sought to write a book of information, explanation and inspiration: there was so much to say and so little time. For helping me to see the wood for the trees, I thank my husband, Harry Arthurs, who read my manuscript as it was taking form and often showed me the error of my ways, and Liz Primeau, who knew exactly where and when to prompt me to do it better. Thanks also to professional colleagues: to Beryl West, for her patience as my sounding board and for her fine work in looking after the gardens we make together; and to Bruce MacLean and Dirk Wentzel, who built some of the gardens featured in this book, for their intelligence and unstinting pursuit of excellence and for their friendship. I have greatly appreciated the support of Wanda Nowakowska at Madison Press who makes a deadline sound like an invitation to dinner; working with her has been a pleasure indeed. On the home front, warmest thanks to my family and specially to my father from whom I inherit my passion for gardens.
— *Penny Arthurs*

❧ You wouldn't be reading this book if it weren't for Penny Arthurs, a respected garden designer who's also a font of original ideas and has the ability to express them well. She's written a wonderfully readable, helpful and inspirational book, and I'm indebted to her for it. I'd also like to express my appreciation to Wanda Nowakowska, Madison Press assistant editorial director and the project editor for this series; her vision and dedication, her tact and good humor make it a pleasure to work with her. My thanks, too, to Brenda and Trevor Cole for passing their careful eyes over the text, and to all the photographers from across the country who so willingly submitted their work for this project. Gordon Sibley's elegant design and choice of type faces have given the whole series class. All of us who worked on this book appreciate the support of *Canadian Gardening's* editorial director, Tom Hopkins, and our publisher, Phil Whalen.
— *Liz Primeau*

The map of Canada's Plant Hardiness Zones (pages 88-89) was produced by the Centre for Land and Biological Resources Research, Agriculture Canada, from information supplied by the Ottawa Research Station and the Meteorological Branch, Environment Canada 1993. We would like to thank Bryan Monette and Ron St. John of the Research Branch for their kind help in supplying this material.

INDEX

EDITORIAL DIRECTOR   Hugh Brewster

PROJECT EDITOR   Wanda Nowakowska

PRODUCTION DIRECTOR   Susan Barrable

PRODUCTION COORDINATOR   Sandra L. Hall

BOOK DESIGN AND LAYOUT   Gordon Sibley Design Inc.

PRINTING AND BINDING   Tien Wah Press

CANADIAN GARDENING'S
SMALL- SPACE GARDENS
was produced by
Madison Press Books